BUSINESS, BUSINESS, BUSINESS!

The Entrepreneur's Guide to Strategies, Secrets and Savings

John Livingstone
Serial Entrepreneur

BusinessBusinessBusiness.biz

88Publications.com
7040 Avenida Encinas, Suite #10488
Carlsbad, CA 92011 U.S.A.

Ordering Information:

Orders from individuals, U.S. trade bookstores, and wholesalers, please visit **www.BusinessBusinessBusiness.biz.**

Overseas orders: **www.88Publications.com.**

Quantity sales. Special discounts are available on quantity purchases by corporations, associations, schools, and others. For details, contact the publisher at the address below.

Copyright © 2014 by John Livingstone/88 Publications

All rights reserved. No part of this publication may be reproduced, distributed, or transmitted in any form or by any means, including photocopying, recording, or other electronic or mechanical methods, without the prior written permission of the publisher, except in the case of brief quotations embodied in critical reviews and certain other noncommercial uses permitted by copyright law. For permission requests, write to the publisher, addressed "Attention: Permissions Coordinator," 88 Publications, 7040 Avenida Encinas, Suite #10488, Carlsbad, CA 92011 U.S.A.

Important Notice:
All prices from third parties referenced in this book were accurate at the time of publishing and are subject to change.

This book is intended to provide strategies, secrets and savings based on the real life experiences and opinions of serial entrepreneur John Livingstone and in no way is intended as legal or accounting advice. Please contact an experienced attorney or professional accountant for legal and accounting advice.

Every effort has been made to provide accurate and dependable information. The author, editors, and publisher cannot be held responsible for any error, omission, professional disagreement, outdated material, or adverse outcomes that derive from any use of the strategies, secrets, savings, or ideas contained in this book.

All brand names, product names, Registered names, or Trademarks are used for journalistic or editorial purposes only, and belong to their respective owners. BUSINESS, BUSINESS, BUSINESS! has no ownership and does not intend to imply any relationship.

BUSINESS, BUSINESS, BUSINESS!

The Entrepreneur's Guide to Strategies, Secrets and Savings

Advance Praise from Fellow Entrepreneurs

"I have known John Livingstone for almost 10 years. On one occasion, I had just purchased a new office building, but was not sure how I would use it. John recommended an executive office rental business. I trusted him to help me. John designed the layout, oversaw construction, and gave me marketing advice. Soon all of the offices were leased and to this day the business provides me with a great income. Many other times, when I needed some business advice, whether it is about websites, lease negotiations, personnel, or almost anything else, I have called John and he always has the best answer."

- Sonya Orme
President, Prime Executive Offices, Inc.

"Many years ago, I had the pleasure of meeting John Livingstone. I was impressed with his entrepreneurship skills. I have trusted John on numerous occasions for advice, as well as his business acumen. John has assisted me with negotiating my office lease, finding a buyer for an out of state property, providing accounting advice, and other matters. John is the first person I think of when I have a business question."

- Dr. Joseph Castrejon

"It was while working on a complex legal matter that I met John Livingstone. I have learned that John is a true entrepreneur. He is one of the smartest men I know. His ability to comprehend complicated situations requiring a good understanding of the legal issues is something I have seen in John. I am sure readers of this book will find a great deal of very useful information on how to launch and build a business."

- Conrad F. Joyner Jr., Attorney-at-Law

"Since I met John Livingstone, I have come to know him as the ultimate entrepreneur. He has innovative ideas, follows through on his ideas, and completely understands customer service. It is a pleasure to know John, both as a businessman and a friend."

- Dr. James Kline

Acknowledgements

I would like to thank you, my readers, even though we may not have met. We are kindred spirits, who have escaped the monotonies of life, to journey as entrepreneurs taking risks and enjoying the excitement of launching and building businesses.

It is important that I thank the love of my life, Kelly Ann, also an entrepreneur, who has been 100% supportive of my endeavors. She has traveled with me through the pain and joy of entrepreneurship and I love and thank her for sharing her life with me. On this book, her research and copy editing have been critical to any success.

I am also grateful to the many people who took the journey with me through this book; to those who provided inspiration, talked things over, offered comments, allowed me to quote their remarks, and assisted in the editing, proofreading, and design.

Editing and Proofreading: Martin J. Coffee
                                    Coffee2go Editing Solutions

Cover Design: Introsudio.me

Table of Contents

Introduction		i
Chapter One	Never a Paycheck	1
Chapter Two	SWOP Analysis – a Mandatory Research Tool!	7
Chapter Three	Choosing a Company Name and Logo – Trademarks and Patents	29
Chapter Four	Cash to a Business is Like Blood to a Human	37
Chapter Five	Developing the Team of Advisers that is Right for You	55
Chapter Six	Think Smart – the Right Decision for a Business Location	67
Chapter Seven	Mediocre Employees = Mediocre Business	83
Chapter Eight	Trust Your Gut, Be on the Leading Edge, Not the Bleeding Edge	95
Chapter Nine	Growing Your Business – Be a Killer Competitor	105
Chapter Ten	Without Sales, Nothing Else Matters	125
Chapter Eleven	Design, Prototypes, and Contract Manufacturing	139
Chapter Twelve	Free or Cheap Marketing and Branding	147

Chapter Thirteen	Social Media and Marketing Your Business	157
Chapter Fourteen	Free Websites and Maximizing Their Effect	165
Chapter Fifteen	Finding Overseas Suppliers	173
Chapter Sixteen	An Exit Plan and Some Interesting Choices	183
Appendix A –	Domain Names and Owners Referenced in BUSINESS, BUSINESS, BUSINESS!	189
Appendix B –	Example of SWOP Analysis	194
Appendix C –	Test for Prospective Employees	199

Introduction

You have a great idea for a business, or are already operating a growing business, and need some business guidance to further your success. The strategies, secrets, tips, and money-saving ideas discussed in this book will apply to almost every type of business – from a home-based freelancer, a retailer, a manufacturer, a professional and a person with an entrepreneur-driven high-tech startup looking for guidance on how to raise money and to carefully invest the initial funding of the business.

This book is not intended for successful, well-established entrepreneurs with mature businesses, as they have surely already applied many of the strategies I discuss. However, entrepreneurs are always curious about how others have built businesses, so you too are welcome to read on.

The knowledge I am sharing comes from 40 years in the trenches launching and building businesses. I am conveying this information in an easy-to-read, non-technical, and often simplistic way so that the tips and strategies are clear and useful to all readers, especially the "want-to-be" or new entrepreneurs with businesses in the early stages of growth.

I am certain that entrepreneurs will find very practical strategies and money-saving ideas within these pages that will help you to achieve even greater profitability. Where else will you learn how to obtain high quality, free legal advice from attorneys across the U.S.; the best advice on prototyping and manufacturing; very specific advice on sourcing from China; and many more money-saving tips?

I have also referred to many websites that I have found very useful and that I believe will help entrepreneurs keep their costs under control. For a list of these websites,

Appendix A lists all company names and web addresses, or URLs, with links. The links are not active within the book in order to reduce reader distraction. Printed editions have the URLs, but of course these are not active.

Entrepreneurship, or self-employment, is one of the most rewarding choices you will make in your life. I look forward to helping you lay a solid foundation for reaping the rewards of prosperity and of free time for you and your family.

Chapter One

Never a Paycheck

You have an idea for a business, most of your family and friends support your idea, and now you have decided to launch your own business. Within these pages, you will learn how to build a business efficiently and have the freedom to live life as you wish!

Since the age of eighteen, I have never had a paycheck unless I was writing one to myself. From my teenage years until now, I have always been an entrepreneur. I have a framed clipping on my desk from 1960 in which I was featured in a local newspaper as the top-producing newspaper carrier for new subscriptions. As a teenager, I worked year-round selling peanuts and popcorn at sporting events and always enjoyed the hustle involved as I beat daily sales goals. Often, I had more than one part-time job. I founded my first business, buying and renovating houses, while at university, when I was eighteen years old.

Since those early days, I have started and grown, often simultaneously, a fishing business, a rental car business, a chain of executive office rental businesses, a personnel agency, an advertising and marketing business, a homebuilding business, a mortgage business, a vacation rental home business, and a publishing business, among others. I was creating websites for my businesses, and a few progressive clients, before most people ever heard of websites. I have often been called a serial entrepreneur.

Never having a paycheck has meant a lifetime without a boss, being able to attend my sons' school events, taking vacations when I want, and many other activities that fall under the heading of freedom. I cannot imagine anything worse than being told when to work or what to do with my time, or being terminated just because my employer needs to lay off 3,000 people to raise the share price to make shareholders happy. There is no doubt I have worked plenty of eight-day weeks. I have no regrets, simply because my family and I were benefiting financially and the non-financial rewards, especially personal time, have been terrific.

As an entrepreneur, it is unlikely you will join Steve Jobs and others on the front page of *Fortune* magazine, *Forbes* magazine, or get a mention in the *Wall Street Journal*. Sure, some will, but most entrepreneurs will be pleased to build a profitable business that allows them a good sense of balance in their lives. Being a successful entrepreneur should mean you make more money than you would at a desk in the corporate world and you have personal time for you and your family to do those things that bring you happiness – spend time with family and friends, time for sports, time for buying and decorating a beautiful home, and freedom from the stress of personal bills and living from paycheck to paycheck.

I have often been asked, "When is the right time to launch a business?" First, the obvious – you need an idea for a service or product that will appeal to potential customers in a market that offers you a reasonable opportunity of success. Second, you have to feel the time is right. If you are in a stable job and hate it, then it is probably time to start that business. One caveat, though; you must be able to fail and not hurt others, regardless of how unhappy you are. It would be foolhardy to risk your family's safety and security for your dream. Your family should be your dream.

If you are a single man or woman, without responsibilities to others, then anytime is the best time to see if you are right about your idea. Or, if you believe your spouse is 100% with you on the idea, then go for it. Your family must understand, at all times, that you are not married to the business, but rather a profitable business is a key to family well-being. You are actually putting the family first when some family members may think you are putting the business first.

Maybe you have plenty of money to start, although most successful entrepreneurs have very little when they launch. This makes success taste even better. History has proven that poverty is the inspiration for innovation, entrepreneurship, and financial success. Many businesses have started in a basement, a garage, and even in a pub. If you are a thinker, a hard worker, are disciplined, and are strong-willed, you have an excellent chance of building a great business.

If you have any doubt, there are many well-known names that have started with nothing. Oprah Winfrey is the daughter of an unwed teenage mother from rural Mississippi. Steve Jobs was an orphan adopted by a family without wealth. Jay-Z was born in one of the worst projects in Brooklyn and was selling CDs out of his car. Jan Koum, co-founder and CEO of WhatsApp, sold to Facebook for $19 billion. Koum came from the Ukraine and his family lived on food stamps at one time. Now his net worth is reported to be $6.8 billion. Forever 21 founders Do Won Chang and Jin Sook, husband and wife, worked multiple jobs at one time when they first arrived in America. Now they have 480 stores worldwide and $3 billion a year in sales. And there are many more wonderful stories like these.

Are entrepreneurs born or made? You know if you are an entrepreneur by now. If you are curious enough to read on, you know you are an entrepreneur and ready to put in long hours to achieve success and financial freedom. My goal is to share valuable secrets and strategies I have discovered that work very well, just as any mentor would. Look for mentors, people who have plenty of business experience that you can bounce ideas off of.

BUSINESS, BUSINESS, BUSINESS!

We learn from the experience of others, and every successful entrepreneur has had a relationship with a mentor. Your mentors will save you a lot of grief and legal bills. I realize it is not always easy to find a mentor. There is one great source found at SCORE.org/mentors. SCORE has 300 locations across America and they offer expert, unbiased advice and best of all, it is always free! This terrific service is sponsored by the U.S. Small Business Administration and Deluxe Corp. Foundation. Make it a priority to check out SCORE.

Chapter Two

**SWOP Analysis
– a Mandatory
Research Tool!**

If you are like most entrepreneurs, you are all charged up about your great idea and the most boring thought is of doing some research and planning. No problem. Just be ready to join the 85% of new businesses that fail and suffer the agony of unpaid vendors, angry employees, and government liens and the inability to pay back banks, credit cards, family, friends, and other investors.

To succeed in any entrepreneurial enterprise, you must undertake in-depth research and set your goals in advance. If your business is already established, you must analyze your business and set goals for the future.

Your business needs a thorough SWOP analysis at the conceptual stage, and on a recurring basis. This is a process to identify the internal and external factors affecting the likelihood of business success.

Entrepreneur programs at colleges and universities teach about SWOT analysis, not SWOP analysis. Most entrepreneurs I have spoken with find SWOT confusing, as Opportunities should be considered as Strengths and Threats considered as Weaknesses. I believe SWOT misses the purpose of research altogether by overlooking operational strategies and profitability. This chart illustrates the difference.

SWOT Analysis	SWOP Analysis
Strengths	Strengths
Weaknesses	Weaknesses
Opportunities	Operations
Threats	Profitability

BUSINESS, BUSINESS, BUSINESS!

Once your SWOP analysis is complete, you have a good basis for a business plan in the event you are seeking financing. There are many templates for a business plan, for various types of businesses, which can be found with a quick Google search. SCORE.org, mentioned earlier, has terrific information on business plans.

An actual SWOP analysis for an online lingerie business, prepared by a first-time entrepreneur, can be found in Appendix B.

So, whether at the concept stage, or as an operating business, start your SWOP analysis by thinking about your business in the terms outlined below. Answer the questions the best you can to understand much more about your business. Handwritten notes on a sheet of paper will do for now. The most important thing is to start thinking about these ideas and understanding how strong your business idea really is. If you don't have enough positive answers when determining if you have the necessary strengths, then accept the information. Don't ignore the lack of positive answers.

STRENGTHS – Put your brain to work. Get excited about the strengths of your business. But be realistic. On the TV show *Shark Tank*, you can see the investors groan every time a person looking for an investment makes a statement along the lines of, "If only 1% of the people in America buy my product..." They will never sell 3.3 million units of their product. Those people are usually walking down the long hallway to the exit with nothing but disappointment.

Speaking from experience, I am sharing some strategies and tips for retail, manufacturing, and online businesses. Most of the ideas will be applicable in some way to all types of businesses.

The Entrepreneur's Guide to Strategies, Secrets and Savings

A brick-and-mortar retail business is any business that sells goods or services to others from a physical location. So whether you are selling shirts, therapeutic massages, cars, accounting services, or running a restaurant, you are a retail business if you have a physical location. Internet stores selling merchandise are usually considered online retail businesses.

Retail business – Consider the following when identifying the strengths your retail business might have:

- **Demographics**

Do the residents in your market area have the disposable income to buy your products or services?

Are the people in your demographic area the right age and gender to become customers for your business?

How many residents in your target area will have to become customers for you to achieve profitability?

- **Staff availability**

Are there enough potential and qualified employees to staff your business?

How much will you have to pay staff in your area?

- **Location**

Is there a suitable location for rent or purchase, and at a good price?

Is it a growth area with new houses and new businesses sprouting up? New schools?

Will you be in an area considered a destination? Maybe you need to locate in or near a mall, a major grocery store,

BUSINESS, BUSINESS, BUSINESS!

or a post office so you can attract buyers already coming to the area?

Does your proposed location have easy access? Drivers need to be able to arrive and leave your location easily. If your location is near a subway, then make sure customers don't have to cross a street or have other obstacles to your shop.

Studies show that even climbing a few steps will deter customers. I have a friend who opened a florist shop and for two years there were three steps for customers to climb. Sales were only so-so. I encouraged her to move two doors away to a shop that had no stairs. Sales increased 300% the next year and have continued to grow.

- **Signage**

Is signage going to be visible? Look for good places for your signs. Will trees or wires block your signs? Is it likely large vehicles such as buses and trucks might block your signs for a large part of the day? Walk and drive by your proposed location and study this carefully. Banks and supermarkets prefer corner locations for the high visibility. You should too.

- **Availability of product to sell**

Will you be making or manufacturing your product yourself, or importing it? This issue raises lots of questions for a retailer. If you are importing, consider how you will pay overseas suppliers, how you will get your product through customs, and what will be the cost and length of time to achieve this. This topic is dealt with in detail in Chapter Fifteen. Can you source products locally to avoid the risks associated with overseas deliveries?

The Entrepreneur's Guide to Strategies, Secrets and Savings

- **Competitors in the area**

Will your business really be that different? Whether selling shoes or bagels, you must really want to dominate the market to be successful. Ask yourself, "Can my business dominate this market?" "Are my competitors better funded than my business?" "Can I find a location without competitors?" "Is it better to be near my competitors, possibly in a mall?"

The argument for being near your competitors? The location becomes a readily identifiable area for certain products. Think of Fifth Avenue in New York. Luxury goods retailers exist side by side, providing shoppers lots of choice. If you are operating a small restaurant, perhaps you are better off locating in a Food Court where customers go to have a variety of meals. Are you ready and able to create a major buzz about your business that will draw customers to your location rather than your competitor's location? What will that buzz be? If you can't describe it now, you probably can't later.

Online retail business – You won't have the same issues as a "brick-and-mortar" retail business if you are selling a product, but some questions to consider are:

Do I have a solid knowledge of web design and social media such as Facebook, Pinterest, Google+?

Will my products be suitable for selling on Amazon and Etsy.com? Have I researched these and other sites well?

What other sites might I sell my products on?

Do I understand Internet marketing well? Am I up-to-date on the latest strategies for getting near the top of Google's search engine results? What should I avoid doing?

BUSINESS, BUSINESS, BUSINESS!

Can I maintain the website and do the social marketing myself? Or will I have people available with design and technical expertise to maintain my website? How will I locate personnel, how long will it take, and how much will I have to pay for their services? A big fault of many startups is that no one person on the team has the Internet technology experience needed, so a fortune and lots of time is wasted while you patiently wait for the "IT" guys to do as you have asked.

- **Sourcing products to sell**

As an Internet retailer, you will share many issues with the brick-and-mortar retailers. Will you need to learn about importing products from other countries? What are the regulations of various government agencies with respect to importing? Consider labeling requirements, food testing, child-safety, and languages. Ask yourself:

Do I need shipping services and if so at what cost? Have I considered shipping costs to my storage facilities as well as shipping costs to my customers?

Do I need storage facilities and have I considered issues such as having someone to receive shipments from suppliers, security so my products are not stolen, and does my storage facility need to be climate controlled?

Do I have a website that can be scaled up quickly in the event of an unusual spike in visitors and possibly sales?

How will people pay on my website? Credit card, debit card, or PayPal? Have I considered the advantages and disadvantages of all options?

What price will I sell at if I am competing with brick-and-mortar stores?

WEAKNESSES – A SWOP analysis is hard work, but it forces you to remain honest with yourself and avoid terrible and expensive problems in the future.

Some of the answers you discover in looking at the strengths of your business will make various weaknesses clear, however you must consider:

- Cash Reserves – Will you have enough cash in the bank to survive the development stage until sales are great enough that your business is consistently profitable? Be realistic. Your cash reserves are very important.

- Cash Flow – Are all of the sales of your business going to be cash or credit card? If so, it will be much easier to survive those early days. However, if your customers are going to expect credit or "terms," your need for cash in the bank will be much greater. Many businesses make the mistake of thinking that customers will pay according to the terms of 15 or 30 days. In fact, collecting receivables may take up a lot of your time and energy. Be realistic on this point.

- Product Liability – Can your product cause illness or injury? Will you need liability insurance to protect your business? Maybe you are selling gloves; then the likelihood of a liability claim is low. If you are selling food or making a vitamin powder, then you will definitely need substantial insurance coverage.

- Will you need to borrow money? If you do, be careful. Banks often make "Demand" loans which means they can ask you for their money back at any time, even if all of your payments have been made on time. This is common with unsecured loans if you can qualify. Interest costs must be considered carefully.

BUSINESS, BUSINESS, BUSINESS!

Don't count on borrowing from a bank unless you have a house or other collateral to establish a line of credit. If you do get a loan, try to get one that requires fixed installment payments over a fixed period of time. Don't borrow on your credit cards in case the day comes that you can't make your payments on time. Then you may be charged interest rates as high as 30% and your problems will really be compounded.

Ask yourself, "What other sources of funds do I have?"

- Trends – Is your business idea a temporary trend? This is often difficult to determine. At one time, snowboards were considered an idea that would never last. Mountain resort operators prohibited snowboards as too dangerous and now they encourage snowboarders. Snowboarding is even an Olympic event. However, a cupcake shop is probably a trend that will not last long. The tragic Sandy Hook Elementary School shooting in Connecticut on December 14, 2012 caused a surge in gun sales, especially automatic weapons. Many gun owners thought the government would pass legislation that prohibited various automatic weapons, so they created a huge demand for these guns. Retailers responded to the demand by placing huge orders with suppliers. Eighteen months later, some of the same retailers cannot sell all of their inventory and some cannot pay their invoices from the gun manufacturers. Smith and Wesson, a major gun manufacturer, had a share price of $9.92 at the time of the shooting. The stock surged to $17.14 a little over a year later – almost double. When the glut of inventory became well-known, the share price had fallen to $9.18 at the time of writing this book.

So whether trends are caused by fun reasons or by horrifying tragedy, it is best to avoid businesses that are trying to catch a trend.

The Entrepreneur's Guide to Strategies, Secrets and Savings

- Is your business too difficult to start and grow? Proper execution is key and many businesses, even with generous funding, do not execute well. Women's fashion is an example of a very difficult business to execute well with trends changing, many sizes, issues with colors, customer returns, pricing, and discounts to consider. I have not even mentioned staffing challenges. Years ago, a friend of mine had three fashion boutiques. Everyone thought she was so important to know. She was like the guru of fashion in my city, with people lining up to get in her stores. What no one knew, except her close friends, was that she arrived in the store at 4 a.m. to open large cardboard boxes, steamed clothes before putting them out on racks, and attached price tags and security devices. All too often, her staff did not show up. After three years, with her health suffering, she closed her stores. Making money just wasn't worth the hassle to her. Think about the factors that determine the complexity of your business idea. The simpler your business, the better the chance of success.

- How much of your time will be required? It's understood by every entrepreneur that the hours will be long until your business is running well and profitably. Will your family understand? Will you be willing to miss your children's soccer games and school events? Some businesses, such as a home-based consulting business, will not demand so much of your time or you will at least have more flexibility in your schedule. On the other hand, a 24 hour a day restaurant may find you working very long hours.

- Will your business have a large number of staff to manage? If you start a business requiring a manufacturing line, then you will probably need a foreman, shipping and receiving staff, and people on a production line to name a few. Restaurants have plenty of staff challenges. Are you the right kind of person to select and train new employees and to deal with their personal issues in some cases? Do you have the ability to fire people when needed?

- Calm and cool? Can you stay cool in the face of difficulties and emergencies that are sure to arise in your business? Before you say, "I'm going to take a chance," look at your own personality long and hard.

If, after addressing these issues and others pertinent to your proposed type of business, the weaknesses seem too great, then be realistic and move on to another idea.

OPERATIONS

In your SWOP analysis, you must plan carefully for the operation of your business and the financial implications of your decisions.

- What permits and licenses will your business need? Every business needs a business license, however you may need state licenses, tax licenses, building permits, fire inspections, health department inspections, and more.

- What taxes will I have to pay? Some are obvious ones that everyone pays, such as payroll matching contributions as an employer, but others can vary greatly by region. For example, Los Angeles has a business receipts tax for every business. LA's tax bulletin states, "The amount of business tax due is based on your gross receipts generated during the previous reporting period, subject to applicable reductions under City Clerk Rulings." There are some exceptions for new businesses, however current rates for established businesses are $1.27 for every $1,000 of gross retail sales and $1.01 for every $1,000 of wholesale sales.

The Entrepreneur's Guide to Strategies, Secrets and Savings

All levels of government in most jurisdictions will impose taxes that businesses must pay. It is best to have your accountant advise you, before you launch your business, as to the taxes you will be expected to pay and the ways you might minimize your taxes. There is a financial reason why companies establish themselves in tax-friendly states such as Nevada and Texas and avoid tax-heavy states like California.

It might also be as simple as locating your business in a nearby city where these taxes are not imposed.

- Office and manufacturing space – How much space will you need for your office or manufacturing operations? Does it matter which way you face with respect to the sun? Fighting the sun with air-conditioning can get really expensive. Should you lease or buy? Do not over-commit to space. It may be better to rent on a month-to-month basis in the beginning until you know your product or service is in demand with customers. Then is the time to sign a lease for more space, or even to purchase a building. Yes, it would be a nuisance to move; however, it is better than being stuck paying rent on a lease on space you no longer need.

- Leasehold improvements – As a new business, you will have to consider improvements to your space to meet the needs of your business. There are not only cost issues, but also efficiency issues. For example, you do not want your staff wasting time walking great distances to communicate with each other.

It is very important to carefully design a floor plan that will work for your type of business. You don't want your food on display to be in strong sunlight all day. You should probably have your cash register near the door, as studies show there is less shoplifting when this is done. Where will

19

BUSINESS, BUSINESS, BUSINESS!

you accept deliveries? You don't want delivery people, with loaded pallets, coming in your front door with your customers.

- Hours of operation – Most malls dictate the hours the stores will be open. Are you ready to pay staff to be in your shop from 10 a.m. to midnight? Will mall hours force you to be open Thanksgiving Day, Christmas Day, and other holidays? Are your customers going to be in a different time zone if you are operating an online business?

- Products, pricing, and deliveries – How will you get products, store them, process them, price them, and get them to customers?

- Equipment purchases – If you are a manufacturing business, you will need to source the best prices for the right equipment to establish your business. There may be government or other incentives if your equipment is environmentally friendly. Learn from your accountant the effect of amortization and depreciation of equipment on your tax liability and profits.

- Branding decisions – You will also need to make branding decisions, including fonts and colors, and order business cards, signage, create a website and a Facebook page.

- Banking – Make sure you have a plan in place to physically make your bank deposits. You don't want to use a bank that is too far away, causing you to either waste time driving or having to trust an employee to make the deposit for your business.

The Entrepreneur's Guide to Strategies, Secrets and Savings

- Opening day – You will need to consider when you will open your business to customers. Do not open before you are fully ready or your first customers may never come back if they have an inferior experience. Can you have a soft opening when the only customers are family and friends so you can make your mistakes with them? One of the key preparations you should make is to create your policy for refunds, credits, and exchanges and train your staff on your policies before a customer asks. Often your suppliers will take back defective items within a certain time period, allowing you to offer refunds. If not, what policy do you think will please your customer and prevent them from making negative comments to others?

- Customer service is critical – The most important part of your operations is customer service. Consider a training program for your staff and be prepared to lead them in providing great customer service. You must set the example of how customers are greeted, the sales process, and how to encourage customers to return.

I had a terrific experience recently in the town of Evora, Portugal at a restaurant named "Momentos." Wandering along, looking for a place for dinner, we spotted a bright and clean looking restaurant. The owner was outside and greeted us with a big smile and welcome. He told us he chose the name Momentos because he wanted all of his guests to have a "moment" they would not forget after dining in his restaurant. He was spinning a great story and the aroma from his restaurant was so tempting. As we sat down, we were immediately greeted by a server with a warm smile and welcoming words, not "Hi, I'm Maria and I'm your server tonight. What can I start you with?" Instead, she told us about a special Portuguese wine and we quickly ordered a bottle where we might normally just order two glasses. The owner came to our table and told us about his menu and

BUSINESS, BUSINESS, BUSINESS!

said he would custom cook our meals any way we wanted them. He did not have fresh spinach for a salad, but said if we came back the next night he would have some. Sure enough, the next night he had fresh organic baby spinach from a street market. Our meals both nights were outstanding and the fun and ambiance unforgettable. George definitely created "moments" for us we won't forget!

Every review for Moments on TripAdvisor.com is terrific. Every business should take very seriously reviews on sites like TripAdvisor – they can make or break your business. Two examples of reviews you want to achieve as a business owner:

"Best Meal in Portugal"

We ate at Momentos in June shortly after they had opened and I have been thinking about the restaurant ever since! The food was authentic without being too heavy. It was traditional but with a fresh twist. I am not really the kind of person who comes onto the Internet to rate meals, but I would say that this is the best meal we had in Portugal and if you are passing through Evora, you must eat here and meet the delightful owner who will serve you a delicious meal.

"Portuguese Hospitality"

We walked in and were immediately greeted with a warm welcome. The restaurant manager (or owner?) was so kind to explain his fresh seafood purchases from the market that morning. We followed his recommendations and were glad we did! Grilled fish, watermelon salad and wine made for a simple and delicious lunch!

He checked in frequently without being overbearing. I watched him go from table to table making each guest feel welcome in their native language. Excellent service and hospitality!"

Another vendor I use personally in my home is Nick at Integrity Plumbing. A recent review on another review site reflects my opinion as well:

"I find it very difficult to find an honest and really professional plumber...and then I met Nick. He has helped my husband and I in our first home repair which involved a water heater leaking at 1 a.m. He was great with installing it and explained everything he was doing in detail. He also explained that we had a timer on our water heater and that would be a few extra dollars to fix because of a special part he needed to order."

These are just a few examples of the quality of reviews you want for your business. The key is the owner setting a great example by really believing in terrific customer service. Again, your leadership and customer service will ensure your success.

PROFITABILITY

You and you alone are responsible for the profitability of your business. All of your decisions will affect profitability. The hard work of your staff will of course impact profitability; however, you selected and trained them.

In this very important section of your SWOP analysis, consider the following key factors affecting profitability:

- Cost control – You must understand the costs of operating your business really well. You will have fixed costs such as rent. You will have variable costs such as labor and the cost of goods that will vary with sales. Think and plan for these very important factors in your business.

BUSINESS, BUSINESS, BUSINESS!

You might be able to lessen costs through technology. Can a certain piece of equipment eliminate hiring one person? In many cases, the wages for an employee that cost your business $30,000 a year will cover the cost of some new equipment that will eliminate the need for an employee for several years.

In certain types of businesses, you will be selling products that have been imported, or you may become an exporter. Even if you don't import directly, your wholesaler may have done so. In these cases, you will want to understand exchange rates and how a devaluation of the dollar will affect your costs. This can be a significant, yet almost invisible cost, unless you consider this factor in determining your profitability. Again, if these concepts seem confusing, ask an expert – your accountant.

- Maintain healthy markups – Be careful and focus on your selling price carefully. You don't want to have your price too low if your competitors' are higher. If you have no competitors in your market, then you can usually have a higher selling price. This is recognizing the strength of demand for your product or service. The state of the economy should also influence your pricing decisions.

If you offer convenience, then your prices can be higher. Think of 7/11 stores or the pizza guy who delivers a pizza at a premium price, simply because you don't feel like going out for it.

- Optimize your inventory – There are various methods of inventory control, however the key is to only carry enough product to meet your near-future demand. If your inventory is perishable, as in a restaurant, it is critical to your profits that you don't overbuy or that you have a plan to reduce surplus by creating specials. Sometimes you are

The Entrepreneur's Guide to Strategies, Secrets and Savings

better off running out of certain menu items than overbuying and then discarding.

If you have a business with trendy or seasonal items, don't get too carried away with your buying. Retail history is plagued with women's wear shops that failed because what they were selling was suddenly out of fashion and they had a warehouse full of clothes that were out of style. Wine stores are notorious for having lots of "dead" inventory tying up cash. If you are running a seasonal business like a bicycle rental shop, be careful that all of your summer profits are not lost by having to store the bicycles over the winter. It may be better to have an end-of-season sale and buy new bikes the following season.

If your inventory will disappear at a certain point in time, perhaps you are better receiving some revenue rather than none at all. For example, if a seat is empty and the plane takes off, then the airline will never receive any revenue for that seat, so it is better to offer some last-minute discounts. At midnight, hotels will never be able to sell that day's empty rooms. Restaurants often will offer special menu items and promotions to fill seats on an otherwise dead evening.

Selling rooms and seats at a lower price is a form of dynamic pricing used by hotels and airlines. Airlines, hotels, and major retailers are using sophisticated algorithms that utilize game theory, data filtering, and various forms of modeling to establish prices. If you have attended college and studied business, then you may recognize this as Gross Margin Return On Inventory or GMROI. As your business grows, consult with your accountant to fine-tune your understanding of inventory management.

For those of you just starting out in business, projecting profitability requires a simple formula: Revenue minus

BUSINESS, BUSINESS, BUSINESS!

Expenses equals Profit. If you do a thorough profitability projection, you will have a good idea whether or not you should proceed with your business. For existing businesses that are growing, you should work with your accountant to undertake periodic projections that reflect the nature of your business. Many businesses have seasonal characteristics, holiday considerations, and other factors that affect their profit. One entrepreneur I know makes enough profit selling Christmas trees at seven locations each year. He spends nine months a year relaxing in Costa Rica and three months selling trees, and he makes real estate investments each year. The point is that sometimes all that matters is whether or not a business idea makes money. The people who have fancy offices, expensive logos, and surround themselves with administrative staff often will not make as much money, or enjoy life as much, as my friend selling Christmas trees.

The other day in a mall, I saw a business that had just closed down – it was a cupcake shop. What a shame! Perhaps if this owner had looked at the weaknesses and possibility of profitability of this idea, the shop never would have opened.

Let's take a look at what the owner of the cupcake shop should have done. Projecting profitability always requires being realistic with your financial projections. For example, did the cupcake shop estimate how many cupcakes it would need to sell at $3.50 each to meet only the daily fixed expenses? Assume the rent in this high-end mall was $10,000 per month, or $333 per day. Now add in utilities, wages, and insurance for an estimate of $500 per day. The basic expenses total $833 before the doors are open for business each day. Obviously, there is a cost of materials to bake and decorate the cupcakes, estimated at $1.25 each. So if the mark-up on each cupcake is $2.25, the owner needs to

The Entrepreneur's Guide to Strategies, Secrets and Savings

sell 370 cupcakes **every day** just to cover the above-mentioned expenses. Frankly, there are many other miscellaneous expenses that would require the owner to sell at least 100 more cupcakes every day. And, we have not allowed for any kind of salary for the owner – so no paycheck for the owner! This owner will have worked his ass off for 30 days just to pay the landlord, the gas company, the electric company, the water company, the trash company, the insurance company, the flour and icing suppliers, the packaging materials companies, and the employees.

So, it is clear that this cupcake business had a real uphill battle to profitability. But it doesn't mean this owner cannot follow his passion to bring the world's best cupcakes to the masses. The trick is to reduce overhead significantly. Perhaps rent space in a small supermarket, open a small shop in a farmer's market, sell wholesale to local markets and restaurants – do anything except open a shop with such high overhead.

I know of another business where the husband sets up a very small roadside stand on wheels every day around 3 p.m. The stand has four spit rotisseries to cook 24 chickens each day. The chicken drippings fall onto previously peeled and boiled potatoes. He is well known in his area, it smells good, and customers start lining up around 4:30 to make a purchase. He slices a baguette, cuts up a chicken, and puts some pieces of the chicken and greasy potato inside. His wife takes orders and collects the cash. The sandwiches may be less than healthy, but people love them for their great taste! Each chicken has enough meat for eight sandwiches. He charges tourists and locals $6 per sandwich. He is sold out by 7 p.m. and goes home with over $1,100. Even paying for his supplies, he still has a profit of almost $1,000 per day and he works only four hours a day and takes Sundays off to be with his family. He has a beautiful home with a negative

BUSINESS, BUSINESS, BUSINESS!

edge pool overlooking the ocean. Most days you can find Maro surfing until he rolls out his cart.

The point of these examples is that you want to be wise with your time and make as much money as possible. Struggling to build a big business is not necessarily the best idea when a much more simple business can yield huge profits. It's the old adage, "Work Smart, Not Hard."

So get on with your SWOP analysis research the best you can. Get your ideas juiced up and start writing. Soon, you will know if you should proceed with your business idea, and if your business is operating now, start optimizing your business management skills by completing a SWOP analysis.

Chapter Three

Choosing a Company Name and Logo – Trademarks and Patents

I am stumped. What words can I use to describe how important this decision is: Ultimate Decision? Supreme Decision? Utmost Decision? Paramount Decision? Critical Decision? This will be one of your first and probably most important decisions. Don't rush this decision. You will be living with your company name for a long time. You don't want to have to change your name. You want to be proud of it every time you mention it!

There are two approaches to naming your company. First, as a new entrepreneur or small business, you will usually want a name that conveys what you are offering – Mary's Tax Services or John's Fine Shoes. Second, if you have the financing and are planning to build a brand, you don't need a name that will convey the nature of your business. You are planning for the world to know your business by its name only – Amazon, Google, Yahoo, etc.

Based on my personal experience, I have created the following checklist for you to consider before making a final decision on a name. This list also has suggestions that will help you avoid a cease and desist letter or a trademark infringement lawsuit.

- Ideally, keep your name under 10 letters, using two syllables at the most, one hard consonant and repeating letters. Think Google, Apple, Ford, Verizon, Starbucks.

- Convey what your business is offering, unless you are building a brand.

- Name should not be too broad. Not Big Buildings Inc. or Favorite Ski Resorts Inc.

- Name should not be too specific. Not Blue Socks Inc.

- Name should be easy to remember.

BUSINESS, BUSINESS, BUSINESS!

- Name should be easy to spell.

- Don't change the spelling just to get a name. For example, don't use shoez when the word should be shoes.

- Name should be spelled as it sounds to make it easy for customers to remember.

- Don't get cute with some odd name, unless you have a lot of money to establish the name as a brand. If you are building an Internet company and have strong investors willing to build a brand, then by all means get cute. Think Zappos.com and Alibaba.com.

- Use alliteration (same first letter) if you can. Think Coca Cola or Best Buy.

- Avoid initials, hyphens, and numbers. Think Ice-Pack-4U.

- Don't name your company after something personal that no one will understand. No names of pets.

- Do pick a name that starts with a letter closer to the beginning of the alphabet and not the end.

- Go to Google and search your proposed name to see how other people have used it.

- Go to Google and do an image search to see if people have tagged photos with your ideal name.

- Go to Google and do a video search to see if people have tagged videos with your ideal name.

- Do the same searches on Yahoo.com and Bing.com just in case something else pops up.

The Entrepreneur's Guide to Strategies, Secrets and Savings

- Check with family and friends for their opinion on the name. Ask them to be tough.

- Check on Godaddy.com to learn if your name will be available as a .com name. If so, register it. If it is not available, but you really want the name, you can buy it from the owner if it is not being used. On Godaddy's home page, look at the bottom for WhoIs. This is a database that will show the contact information for the owner if it has not been made private.

- Check on Facebook.com to learn if your name will be available.

- Check on other sites you plan to use for availability: Twitter.com, Pinterest.com, Instagram.com.

- Check on USPTO.gov to learn if someone else has trademarked the name.

- Check out LegalZoom.com's trademark service, available from $169 plus $325 government filing fee. They claim to have done more trademark applications than the top 40 U.S. law firms combined.

I have personally found that LegalZoom.com offers great value to new entrepreneurs and small business. Their service makes things easy, provides attorney assistance, and their staff is very helpful. They also offer an ongoing service for $29.99 per month where you can speak with an attorney or accountant on business matters, among many other features. Visit their site for the full details.

I am told by others that NOLO and Rocket Lawyer are competitors that are similarly priced with similar services. There are a handful of negative reviews on all three companies; however, that does not seem too bad considering the volume of business they do.

BUSINESS, BUSINESS, BUSINESS!

If you feel you want to tackle trademarking your name on your own, it is not that difficult. Go to USPTO.gov and follow the instructions. You will save some money. Similarly, if you want to file a DBA, an LLC, or even incorporate, all jurisdictions have information on the Internet that is not too difficult to follow – only time consuming.

Otherwise, I have found when there is big money or a really big idea at stake, an attorney specializing in intellectual property (IP) is the best route. This is definitely true when it comes to patents.

Visit USPTO.gov/inventors/patents.jsp for information on patent filings. Patents primarily are issued in two forms, Provisional and Utility. You will sometimes hear about design and plant patents. Simply put, Provisional patents are good for one year. You need only submit your idea in writing, along with a sketch of your idea. Fees are very low to do a provisional patent filing yourself. The idea is that in the first year, you can explore if your idea has any merit in the marketplace. If you are having success, be sure to file for a Utility patent before the provisional patent expires. The filing must be more professional and filing fees are higher. Again, an attorney specializing in intellectual property is highly recommended.

How can you protect your idea in other countries? Under the Patent Cooperation Treaty (PCT), an inventor can file a single international patent application in one language with one patent office in order to simultaneously seek protection for an invention in the PCT member countries.

Designing your logo. This will often be viewed as the very identity of your business. An option I have used many times is to go to Elance.com.

The Entrepreneur's Guide to Strategies, Secrets and Savings

- "Post a job" and you will soon have many, many responses. Posting the job is free for you.

- You will review the responses and samples of the providers' work.

- Once you choose a provider, they will go to work on creating your logo. With most providers, you can go back and forth multiple times until you are satisfied.

- Once you have decided upon a logo, ask the provider to give you files in formats that can be used for print purposes (letterhead, magazine ads, etc.); a format that can be used on the web; and a format called vector which means you can enlarge the logo for any purpose (truck sign, building sign) without losing shape and quality. Don't stress about learning these formats now as all good logo designers will be very familiar with these terms and be pleased to provide them to you. Ask the provider to assign you all rights to the artwork once you have paid them. Elance has forms on their site to protect your interests.

- Ask for a tiny version of your logo that can go in front of your website name in a search bar. If you are not sure of what I am speaking about, go to CNN.com or almost any other website and you will see a tiny version of their logo. If your logo is too complicated or has too many words, then you may have to modify your logo for this purpose.

- The cost for a logo from a provider on Elance.com is usually $50-$100 and at this price your provider will probably be in Asia, India, or Africa. They work very fast and I have always been very pleased with their work and their desire to please me as their customer.

- There will be very talented graphic designers from the U.S. and Canada who reply to your ad who you may wish

BUSINESS, BUSINESS, BUSINESS!

to use, however the cost is always considerably more and I urge you to conserve your cash so you will survive as a business.

- As your business grows, you may want to change your logo and perhaps hire a well-known public relations firm or advertising agency. There is no problem changing logos in the future, as many companies do this. Some major companies that recently changed their logo include: Facebook, American Airlines, Tazo Tea, Nivea, Motorola, Starbucks, Vitamin Shoppe, Procter & Gamble, Hooters, Instagram, and VH1. Times change, businesses change, and focus studies may prove that existing logos no longer have the same appeal and branding results and thus require updating.

Chapter Four

Cash to a Business is like Blood to a Human

My father always told me, "Your best friend in life will be your bank account – nurture the relationship."

You are probably not reading this book if you are one of those geniuses able to stand, wearing jeans and a t-shirt, in front of a room full of investors pitching an idea that will change the world. For the rest of us entrepreneurs, there are some basics to know for the survival of your business.

As you launch and grow your business, it will seem that you never have enough cash in the bank unless you start at the outset with a very realistic attitude about cash. Your cash will come from these key sources:

- Sales
- Your personal funds
- Funds borrowed from family and friends
- Funds borrowed from banks
- Other business lenders such as hard-money lenders
- Factoring companies
- Peer-to-peer lenders
- Crowdsourcing
- Venture Capitalists
- Angel Investors
- TV Show opportunities – *Shark Tank*, Financial channels

Each of these sources of funds has its own pluses and minuses.

- **Sales** – Your business will sell using a cash method, a credit method, or a combination of both. For now, ignore any discussion of cash and accrual methods of accounting. Your accountant will explain this to you at the right time.

- Cash – generally defined as any form of payment you deposit to your bank account immediately. Currency, checks, and credit and debit card sales fall into this category. The downside is the need for improved security and handling.

- Credit sales – or sales "on account" are sales made to customers who promise to pay at a future date, usually after you send them an invoice. This can be a terrible method of sales since you cannot bank this sale immediately. These customers may not pay as promised, or maybe not at all, and yet you have paid for the product you sold to them.

In my personal experience, I was so pleased when I had my first government contract for a large purchase, only to find that they can take 90 days or more to pay. The invoices often get "lost" on someone's desk and it is not until you call to ask about payment that you will find that the invoice is "lost." My resolution to this infuriating situation, when large amounts of money are involved, is to call my customer a few days after the invoice is sent to ensure they have received it.

I have also sold to large companies, listed on the New York Stock Exchange, that have products in almost every American home and when the economy got tough in 2008, they were the first to arbitrarily extend their payment terms from 30 days to 75 days! We finally received their check 87 days after invoicing. This was in spite of many collection phone calls.

If you are going to extend credit to customers, do a thorough credit check first. This usually includes a credit check with Dun and Bradstreet or a similar agency. Also see if your banker will telephone your customer's bank. Most banks, except for smaller banks in smaller towns, are now reluctant to do this. Also telephone three of your customer's

The Entrepreneur's Guide to Strategies, Secrets and Savings

existing vendors to discuss payment history. Credit check templates are available for free on the Internet.

Above all, if you do decide to extend credit, enforce your terms so you are known as someone that must be paid on a timely basis. For example, if you send an invoice out on July 1 and offer 30 day terms, then you or a staff member should call on July 10 and simply ask if they received your invoice. If they say they haven't received it, offer to send another one immediately and follow-up that they have it. Ask what day they plan to pay your invoice. Then follow-up on that date to be sure a check is mailed. On day 31, call daily until you receive payment. If this loses you a customer, so be it. Well-run businesses will pay on agreed terms. Avoid the headaches of slow paying customers. Also, instead of waiting for a check, you might want to offer to take a credit card payment so that the money is in the bank right away. Of course, you must consider the cost of the commission paid to Visa or MasterCard when you process the payment. But if you are cash-strapped, or the customer's payment is overdue, it may give you peace of mind for the cost of the commission.

- Credit cards – If you decide to take credit cards at your business, then carefully analyze your most cost-effective methods of processing the cards.

Recently, someone I know with a small landscaping business went into a major bank to ask about the bank's credit card processing service. Before he left, he had committed in writing to paying $75 per month for 36 months, plus a set-up fee of $110, plus a 3.75% charge on each transaction processed. The bank person leaned on him pretty hard, explaining that all of his financial relationships should be at the same bank.

BUSINESS, BUSINESS, BUSINESS!

The set-up fee and monthly fee adds up to $2,810 over 36 months and it is not necessary at all! Imagine how hard he would have to work to earn this profit from his business.

There are many credit card processing companies that offer much better rates and service. Some of these include:

PayPal – this well-known company can set you up so you can use your laptop, smartphone, or tablet to process credit card payments when customers present a Visa, MasterCard, American Express, or Discover card. PayPal's virtual terminal option charges 2.9% plus 30 cents per sale and as little as 2.2% if you have a high volume. Numerous other options exist such as PayPal Card Reader, PayPal Payments Pro, and PayPal Here. Visit PayPal.com to determine which program is best for you. They also have an 800 number to easily get help setting up. Since PayPal does not have any startup fees, no termination fees, and no monthly fees, you will save the $2,810 that the major banks may take from your new business.

Square – this company has become very well-known with small businesses as they provide a device that goes in the earphone jack of your smartphone, enabling you to process card payments wherever you are. This is great for farmer's markets, salespeople on the road, or many other businesses. Square's current rate is 2.75% for online sales, swiped sales, or for invoices paid using Square's system.

To be fair, there are several good companies now providing devices for on-the-spot processing of the four major cards – Visa, MasterCard, American Express, and Discover – and all cards are processed at the same rate. Amazon, Staples, and others have payment systems with varying features.

Some credit card readers are also set up to process checks, although it can take several days for you to be able to use the funds since the check must clear first.

What I like about PayPal is that you will usually receive the funds from the sale deposited into your bank account the same night. You only need to link your bank account to your PayPal account when you open your PayPal account.

A word of warning! Just because you get an approval on a credit card that is presented to you, it does not mean that it is a solid sale. If you accept payment with a card that has been fraudulently used, then you will most likely get a chargeback (the money is taken back out of your account). This is why merchants should ask for identification.

I will mention three other companies with which I have no experience, but other people I know have used them very successfully and the rate to process cards is very low. These companies are:

Flagship Merchant Services with a retail rate from .38% to 1.58%

CreditCardProcessing.com with a retail rate from .39% to 1.59%

Merchant Warehouse with a retail rate from .39% to 1.69%

As with any credit card processing system, a bank, PayPal, or other company may freeze your payments if they suspect wrongdoing, or if you don't manage your account properly (too many chargebacks).

Personally, I have never had a problem with PayPal and I am reluctant to make any change that would save me the

BUSINESS, BUSINESS, BUSINESS!

small difference on any sale that I might make by changing processors.

Another feature that I like about PayPal is that customers can make purchases from my company without ever disclosing their credit card details to me. This can be a benefit where there has not been an opportunity for trust to be established between my customer and I, such as with an online sale. It offers great protection for customers when dealing with companies for the first time.

In any event, credit card sales are usually considered cash sales and therefore more money in the bank!

- **Checks** – Checks are usually the worst form of payment, as they can "bounce" and you will have new problems collecting your money. Of course, it depends who is offering the check. Obviously, if the check is sent to you by Hilton Hotels, General Electric, or Wal-Mart, you are safe. However, if you are running a small retail store with unknown customers, you are taking a high risk. Yes, there are check verifying services, but why take on the hassle? My thinking is that if a customer has money in the bank, then they should have a debit card they can use.

- **Your Personal Funds** – Before you have any sales, you will need cash in the bank to start operations and usually this will come from your own sources – savings, retirement funds, credit line on your home, and credit cards. This is often called "bootstrapping" your business. Ideally, you will need only your savings to launch your business. However, the reality is that you will probably be tapping the last three sources in most cases, even if the last three have extra costs in the nature of penalties for early withdrawal or interest.

If you are going to borrow money, lenders will want to see that you have put in some of your own money. This is often referred to as "having skin in the game."

- **Funds Borrowed from Family and Friends** – This is a common source of funds. Mom or your mother-in-law may want to support you in your new endeavor just because she wants to help. Dad might want you to be the next Mark Zuckerberg. Grandma has lots of money and would rather see you use the money when you need it. Friends might be big believers in you and want to be part of your success and be rewarded financially.

Whatever the reason and source of funds, this is usually the easiest money to get your hands on to launch your venture. But be careful. As is commonly known, relationships and friendships are often ruined when money is involved. You should have a written agreement as to how and when the money will be repaid if it is a loan, even if it is one payment in 10 years or another milestone. If it is a gift, then have the gift giver write "Gift" on the check so there is no misunderstanding.

If it is an investment with the expectation of sharing a profit, then have an attorney document this arrangement, complete with share certificates or other documentation. The advantage to you is that as long as you are meeting your written obligation, these people who have advanced funds should not be able to second-guess your use of their money. They might try to give you their opinion, but if your only agreement is to repay the funds, then you have no obligation to listen. You don't need arguments with family just as you are getting your business off the ground.

- **Funds Borrowed from Banks and Other Financial Institutions** – If you are a new business, there is almost zero chance a bank will lend you money unless you have a ton of collateral. You will have to pledge real estate or some other easily sold and valuable asset. The days of convincing a bank to loan you money based on a great business plan are pretty much over for a new business. However, if you have been established for a few years and have a proven track record, complete with financial statements, you may be more successful in borrowing money.

All lenders use the three "C's" in deciding whether or not to lend you money:

- Credit – this starts with your credit score, which will tell a lender about your reputation as a borrower, your character based on number of loans, stability at a job, and residential stability.

- Capacity – this refers to your capacity to repay the loan and looks at your cash flow, debt ratios, cash reserves, and purpose of the loan.

- Collateral – this is what you have to secure the loan to the bank's satisfaction and will usually include your personal property as well as that of your business. You will almost certainly be asked for a personal guarantee, which means you are putting everything you own on the line for your business. A small business will often have to give the bank the personal guarantees of your spouse and partners before the loan is made.

Be very careful when signing a personal guarantee! Ask to take the document to an attorney or at least take the time to consider your decision carefully. If your business fails, the bank will most likely take you to court to obtain a judgment against you. They will then use collection agencies and repo companies that will hound you until the bank is paid back. Personal bankruptcy may be your only option to get a fresh start.

If you do get an approval for a bank loan, watch for the words "demand loan." This literally means a bank can demand repayment at any time. I was in the fishing business many years ago and I had a $600,000 line of credit with the bank that was being used properly. One day, our company banker called me and said the bank was getting out of the business of financing fishing companies and that I had three days to repay the bank or they would begin seizing our building, trucks, boats, and other assets. The banker was not willing to talk about any other possibilities. Fortunately, I had a good relationship with another bank where I did some personal business and they were able to pay off the first bank and I obtained a new line of credit. However, that was a long time ago and relationships with bankers mean almost nothing today. Additionally, these days, banks try to get all of your business and personal banking under their roof.

A survival strategy is to have a second or even third bank where you have some personal accounts so that if your business bank ever lets you down you can easily open a business account where you already have a personal account established. The bankers are never your friends, so don't be sucked into a false sense of security – protect yourself!

- **Other Business Lenders** – Now you are getting into dangerous territory if you are considering some of these sources. If the banks have turned you down and you are desperate for money and have real estate to pledge, you might turn to "hard money" lenders. These are heartless people who are out to take advantage of you. They often operate from their homes and are hard to find. Your accountant may know someone, as they promote themselves to non-professional accountants with whom they often share fees. They rarely will lend you money on the strength of a second or third mortgage on your property; they usually want a first mortgage. The interest rate will make you want to gag, never mind their fees. For example, they might loan your business $200,000 as a first mortgage on your building; however, they will probably only give you $180,000, as they want a 10% fee and your interest rate might be 15% or higher when banks are charging 5%.

The way they calculate interest and other charges may mean you will be paying outrageous costs of borrowing that may sink your business anyway and cause you to lose your real estate.

- **Factoring Companies** – This is a very expensive alternative to banks as well. Factoring companies will take your accounts receivable (the money your customers owe you) and lend you a percentage of your total accounts receivable. They charge fees and interest that rival any loan shark. However, they can be useful in short-term situations. For example, you may have accounts receivable from companies the size of General Electric, Wal-Mart, or McDonalds and you need money now to buy more inventory. These large companies may take more time to pay so you turn to a factoring company that will loan you money today against your future payments from these large companies. In most cases, you will have to provide a list of your accounts receivable and the factoring company will often contact your customer to be paid directly or to at least confirm the debt. While this can seem embarrassing, it generally is not, as it is a common business strategy to borrow money for growth purposes. Just don't get used to this source as it is very expensive.

The Entrepreneur's Guide to Strategies, Secrets and Savings

- **Peer-to-Peer Lenders** – Peer-to-peer lending, or P2P lending, as a source of funding is relatively new. In 2007, LendingClub.com was formed and since that time they have loaned over five billion dollars. The idea behind these firms is that they offer investors an opportunity to receive a reasonable rate of return on their money by being one of many who pool their money to lend to individuals and businesses, also on reasonable terms. For both parties it is a simple process and these lenders have a very good track record of paying back their investors. It is a great alternative to banks.

Recently, Google invested $125 million for a 7% stake in LendingClub.com. Since 2007, there have been numerous other companies start as peer-to-peer lenders. Simply by doing a Google search for "peer-to-peer lending," you will find many sources. Each company has different criteria as far as who they lend to or fund. Most have reasonable interest rates and fixed term loans available.

Some of the best known and respected lenders are:

LendingClub.com – has loaned more than $5 billion

Prosper.com – has loaned more than $1.6 billion to more than 160,000 borrowers

FundingCircle.com – since 2010 has loaned $500 million to small business owners

Upstart.com – a great selection of loans from unsecured loans to fixed-rate loans

- **Crowdfunding** – In the last few years, a very unique and terrific source of funding has become available for many businesses, creative projects, and personal projects. The beauty of raising money on a crowdfunding

BUSINESS, BUSINESS, BUSINESS!

site is that the money does not have to be paid back. However, incentives are offered to people that fund your business and these incentives are generally your products that are being developed. You have an obligation to fulfill these promises.

There are many owners of both startups and established businesses who have raised significant amounts of money on these sites. In all likelihood, your business could raise money on these sites as well. It is hard to believe, but your credit score does not matter, the ability to repay does not matter, and even your character does not matter as people looking to invest simply watch a web page made by you and then decide if they want to fund your idea. If you can imagine an idea, it might well be funded on the sites.

They each offer a couple of options. Once you set your financial goal in place, you can choose a fixed funding or flexible option. With the flexible option you will receive all of the funds pledged, even if your financial goal is not met, less a small commission by the site operator.

I know eight people who have raised money for their small business or a new idea. Each one of them has raised significant money, as high as $325,000. Others who I don't know have raised over $1 million. However, I don't want to mislead you about how easy it is.

Each crowdfunding site offers plenty of advice on how to make your page appealing to investors. You must read the sites carefully and realize that you will only be successful if you make your page widely known. For example, you will want to send a link to your page by email to all of your contacts. You will need to have strategies to encourage your contacts to help you by promoting your page to their friends. A really good video is also wise. This hard work promoting

The Entrepreneur's Guide to Strategies, Secrets and Savings

your page, if it pays off, will get you the easiest money you ever raise and best of all you don't have to pay it back.

Crowdfunding is also a great way to build a huge community of supporters who champion your idea. Often, the importance of community and new networks is just as valuable as any funds raised. The people who fund you will be very sincere, and I believe generally good-hearted people, who want to see you succeed.

Three of the best known crowdfunding sites are:

Indiegogo.com – Self-described on their website as: *"Indiegogo is the world's most established crowdfunding platform. Crowdfunding is the process of pooling money from many different people to make an idea happen. Indiegogo is a way to discover projects that people are passionate about all over the world; where you can take action to help create more of what you love."*

Indiegogo offers two options: flexible funding where if you reach your goal they keep 4% of funds raised, and if you do not reach your goal they keep 9%. So it is wise to be realistic. On their fixed funding program, they keep 4%, but if you do not reach your goal then all funds are returned to the contributors.

A campaign on Indiegogo.com is free to launch, you can raise funds for almost any purpose, and there is no application process. Currently, the site receives 15 million visitors a month.

Indiegogo.com is suitable for a wide range of businesses along with many other types of projects.

Kickstarter.com – On their website, Kickstarter.com offers this information: *"Kickstarter is a new way to fund creative projects.*

BUSINESS, BUSINESS, BUSINESS!

"We're a home for everything from films, games, and music to art, design, and technology. Kickstarter is full of projects, big and small, that are brought to life through the direct support of people like you. Since our launch in 2009, 7.3 million people have pledged $1 billion, funding 72,000 creative projects. Thousands of creative projects are raising funds on Kickstarter right now."

If your project is successfully funded, Kickstarter.com applies a fee of 5% to funds raised. This site is targeted to those raising funds for creative endeavors, so it would not be suitable for raising funds for most restaurants or other businesses.

GoFundMe.com – This is very popular, however the primary purpose is to raise funds for personal reasons such as to pay for an operation or to replace a fire-damaged home.

- **Venture Capitalists** – Most entrepreneurs will never meet venture capitalists. Generally, venture capitalists are interested in startups that have huge potential to disrupt the established way of doing business in a certain field. Getting the attention of a venture capitalist for your idea is the first challenge, as most venture capitalists report getting hundreds, if not thousands, of submissions from people seeking funding for a wide variety of businesses. In fact, people often speak about having an elevator pitch. This means being able to explain your business to a venture capitalist in the time it takes to ride up an elevator to his office. Obviously this is probably not something you will ever do, but it gives you an idea of the intensity of trying to make a pitch for funds. You can read interviews with various venture capitalists in business publications and they will all say that only one of 10 or maybe one of 100 investments worked out well for them.

These venture capitalists will always want a significant portion of your equity in exchange for funding. They are hoping that one day your business will go public and those shares bought in the early stages will be worth a fortune. Facebook may be the best example of this method of raising funds and venture capitalists received billions of dollars when Mark Zuckerberg took the company public.

Every entrepreneur dreams big, so if you think your business or idea will be of interest to venture capitalists, your best bet is to Google the name of your city and "venture capitalists." Then for a wider selection and all the top names, Google only "venture capitalists." Wikipedia will be in the search results and they also have some international names. Several magazines publish the Top 10, Top 20, and Top 50 venture capitalists. Try to identify their interests before wasting your time. For example, some specialize in solar applications and others ignore solar applications. Keep in mind you will have to be very well prepared in making any presentation to venture capitalists if you are fortunate enough to obtain an appointment.

- **Angel Investors** – By definition, angels are high net worth individuals who invest their own money in exchange for an equity share of your business. The two main differences between an angel investor and a venture capitalist are first, that angels invest their own money and venture capitalists generally invest someone else's money, and second, angels usually make smaller investments starting at $5,000 and venture capitalists usually start with investments in the millions of dollars.

Angel investors make investments in a wide range of businesses: technology startups, biotech, medical devices, life sciences, consumer products, Internet, telecommunication, information technology, business services, financial services,

BUSINESS, BUSINESS, BUSINESS!

media, environmental, healthcare services, and industrial technology among others.

Before approaching angel investors, your business should have some traction in the form of sales and customer demand.

To start your search for an angel investor, visit AngelCapitalAssociation.org/directory or the Angel Resource Institute at AngelResourceGroup.org.

- **TV Shows** – This is such a remote possibility for most entrepreneurs. While the TV show *Shark Tank* is wildly popular, and I hate to miss an episode, the fact is that huge numbers of people apply and only a few make it onto the show. In 2012, there were 36,076 hopeful entrepreneurs. However, those who are successful may receive an investment. *TV Guide* reports that as of December 2012, investments by the sharks totaled $12.4 million. Other networks, including CNBC, have started segments on their day-time financial programs that put entrepreneurs in front of investors.

As you see, it can be hard work to raise funds for your business. Now, DON'T WASTE THE MONEY!

Remember, this cash you raise will be the blood that keeps your business alive.

In the following chapters, I will share with you more secrets and strategies I have learned to make sure money is not wasted in really stupid ways.

Chapter Five

Developing the Team of Advisers that is Right for You

Don't let any adviser smooth-talk you, or scare you. Hire your advisers wisely at the beginning to conserve your cash. They will, of course, expect to be paid and you should only hire them as actually needed.

You will need to hire a bookkeeper from the outset, even before your first sale, so your cash can be tracked properly. This person will have lots of good advice on how to operate your business and will tell you which accounts to open with the IRS, state authorities, and others.

If you don't have a good understanding of basic bookkeeping and accounting, I strongly recommend you visit KhanAcademy.org, which offers free and easy to understand video courses on almost every subject. Look for Accounting and Financial Statements. There are excellent videos on the three most important financial statements for any business: balance sheets, cash flow statements, and income statements. After watching these videos, you will have some basic understanding when talking with your bookkeeper and accountant.

Asking a business friend for a referral is often the best method of finding a bookkeeper. If you're not able to obtain a personal referral, then do a Google search or check Craigslist.org, which might offer some good leads. Always ask a potential bookkeeper for at least three referrals to unrelated, current clients and then talk to them!

Remember, your bookkeeper will be handling your money, so you want to do everything possible to make sure they are trustworthy. In my fishing business, there was lots of cash every day, just like many retailers today. My policy was to personally oversee the counting of the cash from each store and at the end of the day watch the bookkeeper enter the amounts onto a deposit slip which would then be taken to the bank. This was a longstanding practice and one day, for some reason, when the bookkeeper was making up the deposit, I glanced at the copy of the previous day's deposit that had been stamped by the bank. It struck me that something was wrong about the dollar amount. I asked the bookkeeper about the dollar amount and she acted like I was crazy and became offended that I was questioning her. She told me that sometimes she put two days of cash receipts on one page.

I told her I would take the deposit she had just made up to the bank the next day. As soon as she left the office, I tried matching the copies of the deposit slip to the special bank statement that I had obtained from the bank. They all matched, but I was still certain that something was wrong. I looked very carefully at the deposit book and when I forced open the staples that bound the deposit book together, I discovered bits of the duplicate deposit slip that she had torn out. It seemed that eight duplicate deposit slips were missing. I also took a completely blank deposit slip book and tore it apart and it had eight more slips than the book we were using for our deposits, thereby confirming eight missing deposit receipts.

It was obvious she had been stealing from me for a long time. As the evening passed, I then took all of the sales reports from the stores for the same period as the deposit book covered and sure enough, the sales had been $60,000 more than was put in the bank. She had not only taken $60,000, but also this had been going on for several years. However, she had destroyed the old deposit books instead of keeping them safe as part of our records. I called my attorney at home and he immediately told me that I had to call the police. I did and the next morning the police arrived and questioned her. She immediately broke down and confessed. She was convicted, went to jail, and was ordered

The Entrepreneur's Guide to Strategies, Secrets and Savings

to pay me back. Thirty years later and I am still waiting for the first payment.

I have asked myself so often how this could have happened to me. It's a poor excuse, but at the time I was extremely busy working 80+ hours a week finding enough fish for my stores, staffing my stores, doing the marketing, placing advertisements, and trying to take care of administrative matters and I was robbed by a trusted employee.

On another occasion, about ten years ago, I was in the office reconciling my bank statements on a sunny Sunday afternoon. I was questioning my sanity for being in the office rather than outside enjoying the day with family and friends. The task was quite routine, and more than anything I was analyzing my checks and wondering if I really needed to spend money on certain expenses. Suddenly, I saw several entries that made no sense. I looked at the corresponding canceled checks that were enclosed with the statement and did not recognize the writing, the payee, or the amounts. There was $4,200 in checks payable to a major department store and on the back were markings showing the checks had been exchanged for cash. I was dumbfounded at how this could happen.

I pulled out the checkbook, a large book with three blank checks on each page and corresponding stubs. I looked at the check numbers of the cashed checks and the numbers were from the back of the checkbook. The stubs and checks were missing. I had absolutely no idea who could have done this.

I kept this checkbook, and several other checkbooks, in my desk drawer in my private office. As a matter of practice, I never allowed anyone to be in my office unless I was present. However, we were in an office park in the Arizona

BUSINESS, BUSINESS, BUSINESS!

desert and the management company had hired a pest control company to spray around the building, including the offices, for scorpions and other bugs. Unbeknownst to me, my assistant allowed this man to enter my office to spray.

On legal advice, we could not accuse him or his company without evidence. I contacted the general manager of the department store where the checks were cashed and they were able to find videotapes for the days that the $4,200 of checks were cashed. There he was in his pest control uniform cashing my checks. It also turned out that the cashier was a relative of his who worked in the department store and so he was not asked for identification. Both of them had lots of legal problems after that day.

Even now, many years later, I still receive paper statements from the banks, print copies of the cancelled checks, use deposit books that I inspect if someone else makes the deposit, and I make the time to reconcile the bank accounts personally. I know of three other presidents of large construction companies who approve every check before it goes out electronically, as well as reviewing bank reconciliations that are prepared by their staff.

How far you want to go to protect yourself and your money is up to you.

At the outset, you should also select a CPA who will have advice on matters such as operating as a sole owner, partner, or corporation. Your bookkeeper will prepare your books for your CPA. From these records, the CPA will file your taxes and can probably refer you to a business attorney if a partnership or corporation is needed. Remember, do not spend a lot of money on these services in the early stages if you are starting a relatively small business. You do not need a big accounting firm when a local CPA, who is a sole practitioner, can meet your needs at a very reasonable price.

The Entrepreneur's Guide to Strategies, Secrets and Savings

Selecting the right attorney for your business is a little more difficult. If you're truly a small business, perhaps run by you and your spouse, then you should probably hire an attorney in your neighborhood. Call the law office in advance and ask if their attorney handles business matters. If so, ask for a meeting to see if the two of you will be a good fit. Go to the meeting with a list of questions about starting a new business. The key question to discuss is how you should operate your business – as a sole proprietorship, a partnership, or corporation? If you're efficient, this meeting should take no more than 30 minutes and in many states attorneys will provide you with 30 minutes of advice at no cost. Ask if there will be any charge or fees when setting an appointment.

You have many choices when gathering information about legal options. One of my favorite sources for legal documents is LegalZoom.com. For most business documents such as purchase orders, commission agreements, employment contracts, employee handbooks, and RFPs (Requests for Proposals), you can find good templates online.

Avvo.com is a real money saver for small businesses. This website is free to join. You can ask any legal question and lawyers will respond with answers **at no cost to you**! I have used Avvo.com many times and there does not seem to be a limit to how often you can ask a question. To get good answers, you must carefully ask your question. Start with the state you are doing business in so that an attorney from that state can answer with specifics. The nature of the problem should be short and go in the title section. For example, "California – can I fire an employee for wearing inappropriate clothing?" This lets attorneys quickly see if this is their area of expertise. Further down on Avvo.com's web page, you can expand on the facts so you will get the best answer possible. Interestingly, the attorneys will sometimes challenge each other and you will find that other attorneys will join in, leaving you with the correct legal advice. It works. If you need further advice, the attorney is available once you agree on fees. I have found each time that the free advice was more than enough to make a decision.

If you have a minor legal problem, another alternative is to go to Craigslist.org for an attorney who will work on a piecemeal basis. Google search for Craigslist and your city name. Then from the index go to Service and select Legal. Obviously an attorney who advertises on Craigslist will not have the resources of a big firm attorney, however they may suit your needs.

Someone I know recently had a legal problem and his firm's regular attorney wanted a retainer of $5,000. So I recommended he look on Craigslist and he found a semi-retired attorney who agreed to take on the whole task for $250. Essentially, this attorney took direction from my friend and managed all the documents to be filed, as well as giving great advice. He really does not care if his regular attorney is unhappy with this arrangement! He saved at least $4750.

Another source of legal assistance is a paralegal. They tend to operate in a grey area of not being able to give legal advice. However, the simple act of completing some documentation correctly requires them to have some legal knowledge, which might be sufficient for your immediate purpose. It can't hurt to call several paralegals in your area and discuss your needs and their services and rates.

For example, an acquaintance of mine was sued by a supplier of some merchandise. This acquaintance had ordered $4,000 of leather belts which turned out to be very poor quality and she refused to pay. The supplier sued her. Her attorney wanted $3,500 as a retainer, which obviously was not going to work. My acquaintance turned to me for ideas. I suggested she Google paralegals in her area and then call some and see what could be done to help. She contacted a very helpful paralegal who in turn created a legal "Response" to the lawsuit. They continued to work together until the supplier gave up the legal fight and sent a truck for his merchandise. The total cost of the paralegal was $450. My acquaintance saved $3,050 in legal costs.

Now if you are launching a larger business or trying to grow your existing business, then a fully qualified attorney is mandatory as part of your team. Generally if your business is of this size, you will have met attorneys with whom you feel comfortable. But please be careful to avoid wasting your firm's money on fast-talking attorneys who will tell you of all the horrible things that will happen to you and your business unless you follow their advice. Remember how hard it was to make the money you have in the bank and that every excessive dollar you pay an attorney is coming right out of your pocket.

Once you select an attorney or a firm of attorneys to meet your needs, always determine the fee arrangement upfront. Set milestones and fees. For example, to file a lawsuit for copyright infringement, determine an amount that will be paid to the attorney to create the documents and file at the courthouse. Then determine how much a day of deposition will cost, including estimated transcription costs. Discuss the number of depositions. Ask how much each court appearance will cost. Even ask if he charges for travel time. Finally, ask the attorney if there are any other costs that have not been discussed. If you do not determine these things in advance, then you can only blame yourself when you get an invoice for $15,000 and there is a list of items for "research" and "consulting with associates" to name just a few items that are used to pad the bill you are given. And if

BUSINESS, BUSINESS, BUSINESS!

you cannot afford to pay this attorney, you have a new major problem. This happens every day to entrepreneurs who don't know enough to ask questions at a time of emotional stress.

As a startup company, you must watch these expenses very carefully. You will get lots of people telling you about legal steps to take. Many of these steps will be really good advice, but you must think carefully for yourself if you really need to take the step. Maybe put your question on Avvo.com first and then if the responding attorneys advise you to see an IP attorney, then you probably have an issue that is complex enough for more sophisticated advice. Again, set milestones and agree on fees in advance.

Once your idea as an Internet startup becomes better known, and if it is an idea that appeals to venture capitalists (VCs), you will have many requirements for legal advice on how to structure investments and other very important issues. Usually, the VCs will dictate the law firm to be used, although it is always a good idea to have independent legal advice. The fact of the matter though is that the VC has the money you need and once they are an investor, your business will usually become a client of the firm they recommend. Setting milestones and fees will be out of your hands. Besides, at this point you should be focusing on getting your business established.

There are many really cool programs or apps that can make the legal aspect of your business much easier if you have a lot of paper to handle. Two of my favorites are:

1) Docusign.com – this company describes themselves as: *"DocuSign is a San Francisco- and Seattle-based company that provides electronic signature technology and Digital Transaction Management services*

The Entrepreneur's Guide to Strategies, Secrets and Savings

for facilitating electronic exchanges of contracts and signed documents." This is a great tool for quickly handling documents that need to be signed. At this time, the company says 40,000 new users join daily for a current total of 40 million clients. You can use the service on any device and the cost at present is only $10 per month and you can try it for free for 14 days.

2) TurboScan – You can download this app from iTunes and Google Playstore. In these days when a fax machine is as dead as a typewriter, it is great because it allows you to scan and file multiple page documents right from your mobile device. The documents can be emailed and managed in many ways. The app is only $3.99. It is one of my best business tools and I recommend it to everyone.

The third member of your professional advisory team will be your insurance broker or agent. This person may be your most valuable resource as you grow your business. You may need property insurance, liability insurance, insurance on shipments, and even health insurance as determined by the type of business you operate. Depending on the area, insurance agents are licensed to provide certain kinds of insurance. This may require you having more than one insurance agent. For example, construction liability insurance would normally be offered by someone different than someone offering health insurance.

Generally, the broker tries to determine your needs and gets quotes from various insurance companies. As with anything, there will be pluses and minuses to each option. Your bookkeeper or CPA can discuss your immediate needs as an entrepreneur. For example, if you are selling food or a product that may cause illness or injuries, you will need some form of comprehensive liability insurance. Once you hire employees, you will need workers' compensation insurance.

BUSINESS, BUSINESS, BUSINESS!

This is often available through local governments as well as private insurance.

Chapter Six

Think Smart – the Right Decision for a Business Location

Think and act smart! Depending upon the type of business you are starting, there are many options available to the new entrepreneur that will protect you and your business into the future. You might be starting out in your home or garage, but as you grow you will need to understand your options. To protect yourself, you must think smart.

- **Negotiate Wisely** – A few years ago, a friend of mine named Prisco, who is an incredible Italian chef, wanted to open a new restaurant. This beautiful new mall was opening and he wanted to open his restaurant in this location. To me, based on everything he told me, he seemed to have found the perfect location. We checked for street traffic count and for projected foot traffic count within the mall, and we determined the perfect space for his restaurant. However, the mall would only be a success if the two major tenants, the department store and a grocery store, actually opened for business. He had a real estate agent, and myself, working on his behalf negotiating with the mall owner's real estate agent.

Prisco was very anxious to secure the location and we had negotiated some pretty good incentives to open the restaurant. The landlord was actually contributing cash to help build out the improvements in the restaurant.

My "brilliant" suggestion to Prisco and the real estate agent was that Prisco begin to pay rent as soon as both major tenants had opened their doors for business. I had seen the situation in the past where major tenants failed to open as planned and all the smaller shops and restaurants went broke paying rent as there were so few customers coming to the mall.

BUSINESS, BUSINESS, BUSINESS!

After some difficult negotiations, the mall owner finally agreed that Prisco would pay no rent until both major tenants were open for business.

As luck would have it, three days before opening for business, the roof of the grocery store collapsed and it did not open for business until 14 months later. The large department store did open and drew lots of people. My friend's business did very well from the start and he never paid a penny in rent for 14 months since one of the major tenants had not opened, resulting in a huge cash flow and profit that made life a lot easier for him.

Similarly, another strategy if you rent a street-front location is to try to add a clause to your lease that says if for any reason the street in front of your location is closed for more than a week due to street construction, or street-front parking is taken away, that you will not have to pay rent during the period access is restricted. Depending on the location and how desperate the landlord is, he might agree. Then in the future, if the city decides to dig up the street for any reason, you will not be paying rent while your customers have difficulty reaching your front door.

Did you know that in some areas, landlords will pay you to lease their space? Of course they must really want you; however, they will often hand over a check to pay for a portion of your improvements, or they may do the improvements themselves and this can be in addition to free rent.

When my doctor needed space, I helped him negotiate a new lease. Due to personal concerns, he was unsure how long he would want the space. I suggested he offer to sign for 18 months with an option for another 18 months. The space had been empty for a long time. The owners agreed to pay cash for improvements, which my doctor did for less

The Entrepreneur's Guide to Strategies, Secrets and Savings

than the owner estimated, leaving him with some cash for other expenses. The landlord also agreed to four months of free rent and that my doctor could take possession of the office immediately. My doctor rushed the improvements and opened his practice almost immediately, effectively giving him five months of free rent.

As is often said, "It can't hurt to ask."

The term, or length, of the lease you sign must be carefully considered. Don't be overly optimistic or unrealistic. Landlords will usually want you to sign a lease for as long as possible. However, if you have a brand new idea, you might want to consider a shorter lease with an option to extend the time. As optimistic as you are, and as sure as you are of your success, your idea might fail and you don't want to be sued for unpaid rent. This is particularly important if you are operating as a sole proprietorship, partnership, or have provided a personal guarantee for the lease.

Personal guarantees on leases are just like a personal guarantee on a bank loan and can financially ruin you or any guarantor. If you fail to pay your rent as agreed to in the lease, the landlord and his attorneys will most certainly sue you for unpaid rent if there's any chance of collecting it. This may mean you eventually lose your home, and if you have had a friend or relative guarantee your lease, that person could also lose their home.

How does this happen? For example, if you sign a lease for 60 months, or five years, at a rate of $6,000 per month, you are taking on an obligation of $360,000. If you pay your rent for two years, and then your business fails, the landlord will sue you for the balance of $216,000, plus legal and other expenses. Try to sign a lease without a personal guarantee and as a corporation. If the landlord insists on a personal

BUSINESS, BUSINESS, BUSINESS!

guarantee, then limit it to something you can handle financially. Realistically, if you are considering a lease with these financial ramifications, you should have a business attorney working with you to at least explain your potential liability.

My good friend is a landlord, and during the recession that started in 2008 she had an empty industrial building for rent. A prospective corporate tenant, with shares owned by a husband and wife, was willing to take the space for five years, but the shareholders did not want to provide any personal guarantee for the corporation. I suggested to my friend that instead of a personal guarantee for five years, she limit the personal guarantee to the first two years of the lease so that she would not lose this otherwise good corporate tenant at a time when it was difficult to find such tenants. She was willing to do this and set a meeting with the tenant. I was at the meeting where this became acceptable to all parties and the lease was signed. The tenant is still paying monthly rent as a corporation and has never missed a payment. This was definitely a win-win for all.

My message is simple. Do not overextend yourself personally until you're certain your business has a proven track record of success. You will avoid a lot of heartache dealing with litigation, liens, and judgments.

Once you have signed a lease, you will probably need to do some physical improvements to meet the requirements of your business.

The most important advice I can offer for this stage of your business is to follow the local laws with regard to construction of your improvements. You will be tempted to cut corners by doing the work without proper permits. Don't succumb to this temptation! If you are caught, your

The Entrepreneur's Guide to Strategies, Secrets and Savings

jobsite can be shut down until all permits are obtained. Even if you get away with it, problems can arise if you have a future insurance claim. Just do it properly from the outset and you will avoid future headaches. Depending on the local jurisdiction, you can often do minor renovations such as building interior walls without a permit, but even then you must know whether you need steel studs or if wood studs will be allowed. Your local building department will be very helpful in educating you.

The second most important piece of advice I can give you is to not go wild with design and materials. Once when I was doing a business deal out of state, I hired a local attorney who had an office finished with beautiful teak and plush carpets and furniture fit for a king. All I could think of was that I was paying for this in his billings. One day when having lunch with a banker friend of mine, I was told that this attorney was a bank customer and that the attorney had borrowed $300,000 to renovate his office – including a private bathroom so he did not have to go down the hall – which gave us both a good laugh. I wonder how many billable hours that attorney had to charge to pay back that bank loan. My point is, don't go overboard, as no one will be impressed. Restaurants often make this mistake!

Near my home there are two examples that illustrate my point. One restaurant looks very nice and has a huge outdoor deck, however I have never seen it even half occupied. The other restaurant has about 40 seats and people stand in long lines every day to be served a meal. Why? The second restaurant offers a nice fresh piece of fish, grilled beautifully, with a nice fresh salad. A tasty and healthy meal! People in this area really enjoy the experience. I have only been to the first restaurant once and while it was okay, the experience was not memorable. The owner was clearly carried away with the décor and a

BUSINESS, BUSINESS, BUSINESS!

complicated menu, yet orders were taken and meals were served by staff that seemed really indifferent.

Lower Cost Alternatives:

As an entrepreneur launching a new idea, product, or service, there are many low cost alternatives to signing a long-term lease while you are building a track record for your business.

If you are able to work from your home or garage, do so for as long as possible. If doing so, it is important to keep up with your industry or field of expertise. Also, join organizations that give you an opportunity to share ideas. For freelancers working at home, join FreelancersUnion.org, a great resource for sharing ideas and much more. One day you will probably have a need to move away from your home or garage.

Following are some great ideas for locations from which to operate your business, while validating your idea and keeping costs under control.

- **Maker-spaces** – These are shared industrial spaces that will allow you access to industrial tools, fabrication space, and other services. One such company, TechShop, has numerous locations across the United States and offers this self-description on their website at www.TechShop.ws:

"TechShop is a vibrant, creative community that provides access to tools, software and space. You can make virtually anything at TechShop.

"TechShop is a playground for creativity. Part fabrication and prototyping studio, part hackerspace and part learning center, TechShop provides access to over $1 million worth of professional equipment and software. We offer comprehensive instruction and expert staff to ensure

you have a safe, meaningful and rewarding experience. Most importantly, at TechShop you can explore the world of making in a collaborative and creative environment.

"Each of our facilities includes laser cutters, plastics and electronics labs, a machine shop, a wood shop, a metal working shop, a textiles department, welding stations and a waterjet cutter. Members have open access to design software, featuring the entire Autodesk Design Suite. Huge project areas with large work tables are available for completing projects and collaborating with others. We also offer a number of experience-driven corporate events developed specifically to bring teams together and engage them in the act of making."

- **Executive Office Centers** – These centers have been around for a long time. Generally they offer a private office within a business office or complex which shares reception and other common areas. These centers are suitable for many types of offices including sales agents, attorneys, insurance agents, financial consultants, accountants, and other one-person businesses. The beauty of these centers is that you generally pay one monthly rent, which gives you use of administrative staff to help you on an as-needed basis. As a startup, this is a great way to control your expenses and avoid working in a home office which is often filled with distractions. And, if you need to expand your business, there are usually extra offices, in the same location, available to meet your needs.

- **Pop-up Retail Locations** – These are temporary locations where a business can operate for one day or for several months. For example, you may be able to rent a cart in a mall for very short term to sell off samples or seasonal items such as sunglasses. The best way to find these opportunities is to contact malls in your area. Often, they

BUSINESS, BUSINESS, BUSINESS!

will provide a cart and some promotion in exchange for rent. This is a great opportunity to test your products, locations, and consumer response in general. Your financial risk is very minimal while gathering valuable information.

There may also be an occasion to rent a larger store for a seasonal opportunity to test your ideas and products. Many readers will have seen Halloween or Christmas stores set up for two or three months. The risk is very minimal, while the reward can be very high if you can negotiate a reasonable rent. Again, contact the management of the mall where you would like to set up. There is usually an on-site office. Discuss with them the possibility of renting an empty store on a short-term basis, a cart in the pedestrian areas, or even a small location on their parking lot. Obviously, you are more likely to get cooperation from a smaller mall, or a mall in a small town, compared with a mall in downtown Manhattan.

Building on the concept of temporary locations there are many new and innovative ideas around the world. BOXPARK is a great example of what is possible and describes itself at www.boxpark.co.uk as:

"BOXPARK is constructed of stripped, and refitted shipping containers, creating unique, low cost, low risk pop-up stores.

"Filled with a mix of fashion and lifestyle brands, galleries, cafés and restaurants – BOXPARK places local and global brands side-by-side, creating a unique shopping and dining destination.

"BOXPARK is not some run-of-the-mall shopping center. It's a living, fertile community of brands packed with talent, innovation and attitude that puts creativity and fashion back where they belong: on the street."

The Entrepreneur's Guide to Strategies, Secrets and Savings

When visiting BOXPARK, an entrepreneur can't help but to get very excited about the opportunity to showcase their goods in such a terrific location. It is full of shoppers, discovering for the most part unique merchandise and restaurants. I cannot think of a better testing ground for many types of new ideas and products.

In San Francisco's Hayes Valley, a really popular "pop-up" called PROXY has a lifespan of possibly 2-3 years until the location is developed. This is very unique as only San Francisco can create. Using primarily out-of-service shipping containers, it is filled with small retail spaces for different businesses, spaces for community groups, and a partially covered interior courtyard. Visitors to PROXY will find food carts, food trucks, re-used shipping containers now serving as restaurants, local art, and even a demonstration photovoltaic array for on-site power generation. Visit www.Proxysf.net for more inspiration and ideas on starting your business at a low-cost.

Las Vegas has "Container Park" which opened in December 2013 and is built on the site of a former Motel 6. "Container Park's small spaces are an ideal setting for new entrepreneurs to test their concepts and ideas which incur fewer startup costs than a traditional brick and mortar shop," said a spokesperson in a *Las Vegas Travel Guide* article.

Container Park has 39 shops, restaurants, and bars with very intriguing names such as Crazy Legs, The Rusty Nail, Wall and Street Art Gallery, Boutiqueaholics, and Cheffinis. To draw shoppers, there is an extensive entertainment calendar ranging from Blues bands to Oktoberfest celebrations. The developers of this concept have created a great opportunity for entrepreneurs to validate their business ideas. Learn more at www.DowntownContainerPark.com.

BUSINESS, BUSINESS, BUSINESS!

To find out if an opportunity similar to the above is in your area, just do a search on Google or call your local Chamber of Commerce or City Hall. It might work for you and your idea.

- **Internet Startups** – Across the United States, there are literally thousands of great opportunities to try and launch your Internet startup. They are usually called "co-working spaces" or something similar. The concept is always alike in that there are options for using a facility that might start with a shared workspace for $75 per month and topping out with a private desk with some extras for $1,000 per month. They usually offer seminars and workshops appealing to startups, freelancers, and other entrepreneurs. Networking and bouncing your concepts off like-minded people is a huge benefit. Rates and benefits vary widely depending on location and value offered. A terrific example can be found at CrossCampus.us, which is a facility in the Los Angeles area. President Obama has even visited and spoken to the members!

Governments at many levels are offering opportunities to startups. For example, New York state is promoting Startup.NY.gov which is for startups, businesses wanting to expand, or businesses wanting to relocate. The big incentive is zero taxes for ten years if you establish in one of ten regions. Benefits also include access to talented employees and great domestic and global access. As a startup, you should check if your local government has any similar programs. However, I would caution you to find out their criteria very quickly to see if you qualify. You don't want to waste a lot of time only to find out your business will not qualify for some reason.

Another opportunity, if you want to learn how to write code for websites and apps, is a terrific resource called

The Entrepreneur's Guide to Strategies, Secrets and Savings

Codecademy, where you can learn coding from anywhere in the world for free. Wikipedia describes Codecademy as follows:

"Codecademy is an online interactive platform that offers free coding classes in six different programming languages like Python, PHP, jQuery, JavaScript, and Ruby, as well as markup languages including HTML and CSS. As of January 2014, the site had over 24 million users who had completed over 100 million exercises. The site has received positive reviews from many blogs and websites, including the New York Times and TechCrunch.

"Each individual who joins has their own profile. To motivate users to participate, the site offers feedback, badges for completing exercises, as well as a function that keeps track of a user's total score and total day streak, and displays it to others. There are also CSS and HTML glossaries available within each tutorial. The site allows anyone to create and publish a new course using a Course Creator tool."

Another great coding opportunity: GitHub.com offers a program for students who want to launch a project. GitHub Student Developer Pack offers students a website name and secure hosting online for a year at no cost. At launch, 100,000 people with student accounts became eligible for the program.

Google also offers an amazing opportunity ideal for entrepreneurs. According to a googleblog entry:

"When entrepreneurs are empowered to dream big and take action, they're capable of tackling significant problems—and they can be an important pillar of a thriving economy. As a former startup ourselves, entrepreneurship is still part of Google's DNA. That's why

BUSINESS, BUSINESS, BUSINESS!

two and a half years ago we opened our first Campus in London, a space designed to help entrepreneurs learn, connect, and build companies. Campus is a hub for the startup community, where entrepreneurs can fuel up on caffeine at the Campus Cafe, gather in our free event space, rent coworking space, and connect with mentors, accelerators and Google teams. So far, we've seen great results at our first locations, Campus London and Campus Tel Aviv. In 2013, startups at Campus London raised more than $54 million in funding and created more than 570 jobs. They've also created great products and services that are reaching consumers and customers. For example, Borrow My Doggy, which began at a Startup Weekend in London and also received funding from Seedcamp, one of our partners, lets dog owners with limited time for walking share their pooches with city dwellers who can't have their own. Eyetease, which created a HD digital taxitop and high-speed WiFi system for taxis, has been a resident at Campus since their launch and have grown their revenue 100X during that time. In Tel Aviv, local community groups have hosted more than 1,000 events at Campus.

"Building on the success of these spaces, this year we've announced new Campuses in Warsaw, Poland, São Paulo, Brazil, and Seoul, South Korea. And today, we're welcoming another new member to the Campus family: Campus Madrid. We're excited to open doors in all these new locations in 2015. Each of these cities has a growing startup community, as well as a Google office so our teams can get directly involved with supporting Campus. We hosted more than 1,000 Google mentoring sessions through our Campus Office Hours Program in London, and are planning similar efforts at our other locations."

The Entrepreneur's Guide to Strategies, Secrets and Savings

Visit www.googleforentrepreneurs.com/ to learn more about the abundance of opportunities offered!

Finally, watch for those rare and truly unique opportunities to launch your concept. One such opportunity that has been offered is the "Shopify Build a Business Competition." Anyone can participate by coming up with a product, opening a Shopify store, and entering the competition. In 2015, at the end of the competition, the five stores that sell the most over a two-month period will win a trip by private jet to Richard Branson's Necker Island for five days of mentorship from Richard Branson, Daymond John, Marie Forleo, Tim Ferris, and guest Seth Godin. And when you need a brain break, you can enjoy complimentary meals, drinks, water sports, tennis, pools, and a Jacuzzi. This is the fifth competition, so if you missed it keep checking for the next one at www.Shopify.com.

Chapter Seven

Mediocre Employees = Mediocre Business

There is a lot of crappy advice out there, such as "There is no 'I' in team." This might apply in some large corporations. However, as an entrepreneur, make no mistake; there is a big 'I' and that is you! As an entrepreneur, you will soon hear yourself saying:

> I have to sign a new lease.
>
> I have to finance a new truck.
>
> I have to pay our supplier or the shipment doesn't go out.
>
> I have to hire a new manager.
>
> I have to go to the bank and try to get a loan.
>
> And most important – "I have to meet payroll."

It won't matter how great your team is if you can't make payroll. Your team will walk out the door so fast and then run to the authorities to make sure they get their money. And you can't blame them – they have traded their time in the expectation they will get paid.

So above all else, remember everything will fall on your shoulders as the business owner.

This is not to say that the team who will help you build your business is not critically important, so pick your personnel very carefully. Start by identifying the type of person you want for the job opening. This is not just a written job description, but imagine the type of person you want in the position. If it is a sales position, then it is likely you want a very outgoing person who is well-spoken and exudes integrity. During the hiring process, put forth scenarios that test their integrity. Does the position require good math skills? Is appearance important? Someone selling pharmaceuticals to doctors may not need math skills,

BUSINESS, BUSINESS, BUSINESS!

but appearance is very important. Someone working at a lumber yard may need some math skills for estimating the number of square feet of drywall needed on a project, but their appearance may not be as important.

There are far too many jobs out there for me to even begin to provide specific attributes to look for. However, think about you and your company first and make sure the new employees will make a valuable contribution.

I hate to say it, but appearance is often a major factor in hiring. A friend of mine is the CEO of a pharmaceutical company and has spoken honestly with me about who he hires. Although politically incorrect, 90% of the sales reps he used to hire were attractive women, as he has found doctors will make time to discuss products with female sales reps, but will ask male sales reps to come back at another time. In the last decade, with many more female doctors, he has also hired some attractive male sales reps to make those calls. When I challenged him on this approach, he explained that his first priority is to educate doctors on his company's products so that his company can maximize revenue and profits. He further rationalizes his approach by pointing out the female and male sales reps, with his strategy, make on average much more than his competitor's sales reps.

Another friend of mine owned a large stationery business before a big box store opened nearby. While still in business, he found that hiring athletic and attractive men to go to offices and sell stationery to the receptionists, who were usually in charge of ordering, increased his sales by more than 50%.

The same friend had a problem in his warehouse. As salesmen phoned in their new orders to be filled and shipped to the customers, there was a huge increase in incorrect orders being packaged for delivery. He could not figure out why for the longest time. As it turned out, his warehouse manager had hired a cute young woman for quality control. So the men in the warehouse (pickers) would pick the wrong items from the shelves, put them in a box, and send them down the conveyor belt. When the cute young woman in quality control would find the incorrect merchandise, she would call the picker responsible to come to the front and meet her to discuss the errors. The pickers would love the break from the monotony of their jobs to go and talk to the cute young woman. And because she was so busy talking to the pickers, some orders were still being overlooked and delivered incorrectly, which meant wasted time and effort to pick up the wrong items from the customers and re-deliver correctly. Weeks later, once my friend finally figured out the problem, it was quickly resolved by a new hire. Incorrect deliveries dropped by 95%. The quality checker was reassigned to the front office.

You won't find these examples in any textbooks on entrepreneurship, but you will face similar challenges with personnel. My point is that there is often more to selecting the right person for the job than is obvious.

In this age of smartphones, you might have a new problem. A friend of mine has a production line at her business. Over the last year or so, it became apparent that employees, particularly the women, were taking more frequent and longer bathroom breaks. So she asked a female manager to visit the women's bathroom periodically and find out what they were doing in there. Her suspicions were correct...they were in there talking, on their smartphones, to their friends and family! This was adding to her labor cost and caused inefficiencies in production. The solution – she called a contractor to come in one weekend and install baffles that jammed any cell phone signals in the bathrooms. Problem solved. No employee dared to complain and now the use of their phones is restricted to the lunch room on their scheduled breaks.

Often, as well as building a team, you have to put more energy into staying one step ahead of your employees. Sad to say, but the profitability of your company may depend on your approach.

Hiring people for their attitude has always been my number one strategy. And for the most part, it has worked beautifully. My second most important strategy is to test prospective employees, no matter how good their attitude. There are many tests available online to help you determine if a person will have the skills you need. My third strategy is to hire people who are ready for a fast-paced business and all the change that will involve. This is true of all businesses, but more so for Internet startups, where innovative ideas and new people will always be part of the culture. Look for people who have a flexible attitude and are problem-solvers.

I have attached in Appendix C a test, and answer sheet, that I modified and use for entry-level administrative positions. The test is a General Knowledge test which will give you an idea of a person's basic math and logic skills. I have designed the test to eliminate those that I would otherwise just have to terminate in the near future. You cannot hire really stupid people just because they have a great attitude. If you do, this person will probably become bored and start asking for a promotion and a raise and matters will just get worse. Hire people you can see as people you will promote in the future. Dead-end people will just hinder the growth of your company. Be tough at this stage. You are not running a charity.

Wonderlic is a terrific company that I have used with great success when hiring for many positions. They describe themselves at Wonderlic.com as:

The Entrepreneur's Guide to Strategies, Secrets and Savings

"Wonderlic develops and delivers standardized, world-class employee assessments for each phase of the hiring process. Our employment tests include job-specific screening questionnaires, cognitive ability tests, motivation potential assessment, personality & integrity tests, knowledge & skills tests and surveys. Used individually, these employee assessments provide valuable enhancements to an existing employee selection process. Combined, they efficiently gather relevant information and provide a comprehensive 'whole person' view of candidate qualifications for efficient, objective employee selection.

"Wonderlic employment tests are based on extensive research and are consistently updated to maintain relevancy in today's fast-paced market. This provides employers with confidence that the tests will have a positive impact on their employment process."

There are many excellent companies that will assist you with your testing procedures. It is very important to your success to spend some money on testing so that you don't waste time and money in the future replacing staff.

Once you have a short list of candidates, invite them, one at a time, to sit with the very people they will be working with so that you can have existing employees offer an opinion about the compatibility of the candidate for the position.

Let your existing employees be part of the decision-making so they take ownership of the decision to some extent. This approach will minimize or eliminate any future problems about cooperation in the office. I have always been surprised at the difference in an office environment when I invited existing staff to evaluate a potential new hire compared to when I made the decision on my own.

BUSINESS, BUSINESS, BUSINESS!

Another key component to successfully hiring a new employee is to conduct thorough reference checks with previous employers. This can be difficult, as many companies do not want to divulge any information about a previous employee. However, you should always try to reach someone in the personnel department of a previous employer and at least confirm employment dates. Another strategy I use is to ask the prospective employee for the names and cell phone numbers of former supervisors and colleagues. Often when I call these people, the information I get is very enlightening and even brutally honest.

Calling customers that the prospective employee dealt with in the past can also provide valuable information. I almost didn't bother doing this once and I was sure glad I did in the end. The prospective employee seemed great. He was personable, his product knowledge was good, and he seemed to know everyone in the industry. He had convinced me that he left his last employer because his commissions had been cut as the company was having some financial problems. I chose not to call this employer as I knew him well as a competitor and did not think he would tell me the truth anyway. However, when I called two customers, I was told the same very negative information. This prospective employee had hung around the customers' offices talking to the staff for too long and worst of all they suspected he had been drinking when he came to the office. One of the customers had even told my competitor about this and that was the reason he had been fired. Obviously this person could have presented big liability issues for me as well as wasting a lot of my time and money.

Finding the best person for the job is made much easier if you can ask around at Chamber of Commerce meetings, and other such meetings, to learn if anyone knows of a good person looking for a job. Networking and word-of-mouth

The Entrepreneur's Guide to Strategies, Secrets and Savings

can be the best source. Some of my best leads came from trade shows I attended. After all, everyone at the show or seminar is in the same industry and may be open to new opportunities.

If an employee is not working out, no matter how long they have worked for you, then terminate them if there is no possibility of re-assigning them successfully.

One businessman I know that has always impressed me has a really tough policy at his car dealerships. Every week, the salesperson with the worst sales is fired and someone new is given a try. This man owns many car dealerships and in every other way treats his good employees very well. A bad employee is like a cancer in your company. They can sink a small business faster than anything else. A large company might have an HR department and programs to help rehabilitate an employee. However, as a startup or smaller company, you have to move fast to get rid of that toxic person.

Max Levchin, a co-founder of PayPal and now Chief Executive Officer of Affirm.com, which offers an option for paying for purchases over time, was recently interviewed for the *San Jose Mercury News* by Heather Somerville and he stated, "I really like running a company. I really enjoy the sausage-making process, where I yell at someone for missing their deadline. I don't like yelling at someone for anything, but the process where you tighten the screws, where you push the train forward and make the train run on time, I like that part." While some employees might find his approach abrasive, Mr. Levchin is making sure, first and foremost, that his companies are successful.

Steve Jobs was well-known for being hard on his employees, but again he wanted to build the best products and the best company. As a new entrepreneur or small

BUSINESS, BUSINESS, BUSINESS!

company owner, you may have to have some of the same aspects in your personnel management style.

I realize in some businesses it is hard to find staff and you feel you must put up with some people. WRONG! I have gone to so many retail stores and restaurants where the attitude of a person is terrible and I just can't understand why the owner has not fired the person – even if he or she is a relative. How many times have you gone into a restaurant and the staff is near the back talking and then they take their sweet time coming to the front and you get a half-assed welcome. That business will never see me or my wallet again. The right person will create an environment that will ensure your business makes more money.

Non-compete agreements are a poor first step with employees for most positions. If you are concerned about your hairdressers leaving and going to a competitor, you cannot stop them. It is better to restrict their access to customers' phone numbers and have a policy against asking customers for numbers.

If you are trying to keep salespeople from leaving with your customer lists, a non-compete agreement will almost never be effective legally. Most jurisdictions will only enforce non-compete agreements if someone is really a key employee and would have access to proprietary information. If you have grown your company to the size where you have a business attorney, you should consult your attorney for the best way to proceed in your area. If you are a small business or cash is tight, consider asking an attorney some questions on this topic at www.Avvo.com – remember it is free to use.

I have always found the best way to keep great employees is simply to treat them fairly. To let them know where they stand, have annual evaluations to clarify expectations and discuss raises and the possibility of more responsibility and promotions. Being open and clear with your expectations is almost always appreciated by employees.

However, sometimes no matter what you do, people might disappoint you. Before he passed away, I had the pleasure of getting to know one of Arizona's most respected general contractors and considered him a new friend. His company built most of the highways and bridges, stadiums, and other prominent buildings in the state. He had long-term, very loyal employees and everyone I knew had the greatest admiration for him. He often shared stories with me. One story that stuck with me was this one. He had an employee that had been with the company for eight years. The employee's father had been at the company for over thirty years until his retirement. The employee, after eight years, wanted to leave and start his own business. My friend heard about this and after all the father and now the son had done for the company, he decided to do something to help the son get launched in his new business. My friend had a gift of a $25,000 check waiting for the son when he arrived at the office to see my friend. He expected the son to give notice and explain about his new venture. However, the son was very aggressive and demanded $8,000 for overtime he said he had worked in the past. My friend was shocked and told him to go see a lawyer. Needless to say, the son's attitude and approach cost him a $25,000 investment in his business.

In another situation, a Canadian general contractor I know had an employee who worked as a project manager on a new condominium project at Whistler Mountain, which is about a two-hour drive from Vancouver. This was an employee with a good record during seven years of employment. However, he had started to be late for work

BUSINESS, BUSINESS, BUSINESS!

quite often. The general contractor called the employee to his office and found that due to divorce and legal bills, he was now driving an old pickup truck which often broke down on the drive up to the mountain jobsite. The next day, the employee was again called to the office and instead of getting fired, as he feared, he was presented a gift of keys to a brand new pickup truck with all the bells and whistles. The employee continues to work for the company to this day and has earned promotions as well. The employee credits his boss for giving him a new sense of self-worth and self-respect at the worst time of his life. Can you imagine the employee's sense of loyalty?

The point of the above information is that you must hire very carefully, provide training and opportunity, know when to fire someone, and make your values known to all so that you are a leader in growing your company. Try to treat employees fairly, don't be taken advantage of, and remember you are responsible ultimately for the effect of your employees on the profitability of your business.

Chapter Eight

**Trust Your Gut –
Be on the Leading Edge,
Not the Bleeding Edge**

The best advice I've learned over the years is to trust my gut when it comes to decisions. I have often been excited about a new concept or product and was almost ready to invest when something in my gut just didn't feel right. After extensive research, and all other signals telling me to go ahead, I still decided against an idea. In business, it can seem to be good to be the first, to be on the leading edge and to get that "first-mover" advantage. However, it can also be a project that will bleed all the cash in your business – the bleeding edge! Sometimes it is just better to watch someone make the early mistakes and then use your cash and other resources to be a dynamite competitor who takes the top spot in the market. Listen to your gut, or that little voice of reasonable doubt, before making the final decision to proceed.

Don't let others feed your doubts! Even as a successful entrepreneur, whenever I start a new venture I am still amazed at how many people have negative comments. I'm not sure what that is about. Jealousy is the most obvious, or perhaps others just like to pull entrepreneurs down. Anyway, I have also learned not to waste more than a few seconds on issues like that. I like constructive advice and new ideas and spend my time thinking about these. People that know me well describe me as very positive. As an entrepreneur, you must think this way also.

Bad days don't mean you are a failure just like good days don't mean you are a genius. You will have contradictory feelings of success and failure and freedom versus overwhelming responsibility. As an entrepreneur, you are different than others, often a loner. These are just your entrepreneurial genes kicking in. You need time alone to think, to visualize the direction of the company. For many years, I went away alone, for up to seven days at least twice a year, to a quiet cabin or other remote spot just to clear my

BUSINESS, BUSINESS, BUSINESS!

head of all the debris of running a business. I would read, write about my business and growth plans, think about staff strengths and weaknesses and my personal goals, and on my return to the office there was always an incredibly positive change.

Years later, I remember reading a *Wall Street Journal* article in which the author interviewed Bill Gates on one of his two "Think Weeks" he took each year. For Bill Gates, this was a chance to look at the current and especially the future plans for Microsoft. Over the last few years, I have met four other entrepreneurs who have similar practices. I highly recommend it as it will bring back the excitement of being an entrepreneur. New business ideas will flow.

Ian Siegel, chief executive officer and co-founder of ZipRecruiter.com, was quoted as saying, "There's really an exciting moment as a founder when you realize the market has embraced your product." ZipRecruiter receives over 2 million applications a month for employment and hiring managers can view relevant applications in one spot.

Many times I have experienced the same exciting moment as I have launched a new product or idea and the first customers started paying my company.

It is often said that entrepreneurs must have passion to succeed. Passion is defined as enthusiasm or excitement for something or doing something.

I have learned over the years that a successful entrepreneur must have a real excitement about his idea or product. This excitement will be gushing from every pore of his or her body! The excitement just cannot be contained. You must be the type to wake up and be excited to build your business.

So whether an entrepreneur is starting a cookie business, or has an idea that will totally disrupt the way business has been done in the past, look for the excitement if you want to experience a future success story.

To be sure I could validate this opinion, I traveled to different areas of the world in the past year. I have spoken with the "want-to-be" entrepreneurs, the newly launched entrepreneurs, and those who are a little more established. I have seen that same excitement I recognize in myself in each entrepreneur around the world.

Like others in North America, I was brought up with a stereotype of the people of China – communism, poverty, poor quality merchandise, and all of that. Of course, I have also read about China's change to a market-based society and the Chinese people's ability to produce high quality goods, such as smartphones.

So this year, I traveled to China to see for myself. I was so impressed by the Chinese people's excitement about having their own businesses and making money. The government seems to create opportunities by providing the infrastructure and supporting new ideas.

The first example of this occurred as I stepped off the plane in Shanghai. For a fee, a man, a young entrepreneur, would carry my luggage and take me through immigration via a special line so I could avoid a long queue of arriving passengers. To see the government immigration inspectors cooperate like this was very surprising. The same man offered to take me to a private car for a ride to my hotel. The car he suggested was licensed, the driver was in a uniform, and the car was a very clean, new Audi. This helped me to avoid a very long taxi line, which after 16 hours of flying was really appreciated. I asked this man how many hours a day he does this. He told me that since it was his own business,

BUSINESS, BUSINESS, BUSINESS!

he often worked 18 hours a day, however he was meeting his goals to be able to house his family in a new condominium, send his children to private schools, and save for a trip he wanted to take to Europe.

At the hotel, I was greeted with more enthusiastic and really nice Chinese people. The receptionist met my car and took me directly to my room where he used an iPad to check me in. No standing in line!

Over the next few days, as I spoke with various staff members, I learned that virtually all of them were working on an idea for their own business. Some were developing apps, some had designed clothes they wanted to sell globally, some had electronic devices that were in the prototype stage, and some had ideas on how to develop new pharmaceuticals and medical devices.

One server stood out to me. She had a Chinese website, but asked me how she could get a .com name so she could sell her lingerie line around the world. She had used her own money to locate and pay a gorgeous Polish model and a Polish photographer so she would have photos for her website that properly show off her work globally. She was also selling her merchandise on Alibaba.com. Her job in the hotel was a way to earn money to fund the growth of her business. Her level of excitement was unlike anything I have seen in another server.

One bartender also impressed me. He found that "outsiders" who came to the hotel did not like the selection of wines. So he researched, and at his own expense traveled to Chile and negotiated a deal to import a selection of reds and whites for the hotel. Hotel management was thrilled to be able to offer these wines. So during the day this man went from hotel to hotel, and restaurant to restaurant, drumming up sales and by night he worked as a bartender. He told me

The Entrepreneur's Guide to Strategies, Secrets and Savings

that every morning he wakes up excited to sell more wine. And of course he asked me if I had any contacts in America so he could import new lines of wine. We currently correspond by email and I will have to see what might develop.

In Portugal, in a small town called Praia de Luz, there were two young Frenchmen who had opened a small bakery to sell their specialties such as smoked salmon quiche, and they sold out each day. They loved their business. In the same town, another entrepreneur had opened a restaurant called YOLO – You Only Live Once. As an owner/chef, he controlled all of the details and the restaurant became very popular within weeks of opening. As we spoke with him one evening, he explained that he had personally done all of the renovations including building the tables. His excitement for his business was on display for everyone to see.

In France, I found numerous people operating small tourist facilities that reflected the essence of entrepreneurship – excitement about their business and opportunities for growth.

Even in Croatia, a war-torn country in 1995, people have purchased boats to offer tourists week-long trips through the Dalmatian Islands where even more people have set up little businesses to cater to those tourists. Cruise ships now dock in several ports and many other entrepreneurs have set up small businesses.

In the Czech Republic, I met entrepreneurs who hand make products to sell on Etsy.com, giving them an opportunity for worldwide exposure and sales to customers from all over the globe.

This excitement can only be felt if you make a decision to launch your business.

BUSINESS, BUSINESS, BUSINESS!

Since you are reading these pages, you probably already know that you are someone different than most others. You are not satisfied with working for someone else and know that you will never achieve your dreams with a 9-5 job.

Your gut feeling in starting a business is the culmination of an internal process that recognized and analyzed an opportunity and then checked the opportunity against your personality and let you make a decision to go forward or to stop.

When you analyze an opportunity, you are avoiding being a foolish daredevil or gambler, but are taking a calculated risk. You have a sound knowledge of your product or idea and a network to help you move forward. You have a strong sense of self-confidence and trust your intuition. You understand the importance of good timing and don't mind being a loner with your idea. In fact, you see it as an advantage because you can be the first mover, if conditions are right, and get a head start on copycats.

You have taken all the practical steps such as checking that you are not infringing on someone's intellectual property and that you are ready to protect your ideas from competitors.

You know how to determine a market for the success of your idea or product. Will your target market offer you a bazillion potential customers? You are careful to be realistic and are not looking too far ahead. Doubts have been dealt with and you are ready to say, "I'm going to take this chance."

Once you have taken this chance on an opportunity, you must be ready for bad days and the feeling of abject failure. It will be time to bounce back and correct your course.

The Entrepreneur's Guide to Strategies, Secrets and Savings

I can recall, as a much younger man, that I thought I had such a great idea and opportunity which involved renting space every weekend throughout the summer. For the first time in 40 years, it rained every Saturday and Sunday for the whole summer! I lost a ton of money on prepaid rents, supplies, advertising, and staff. I have since made a lifelong commitment to never operate a business where there is a significant chance of bad weather. If I have been involved in a sunny weather business since, it has always been in Southern California or Arizona. Lesson learned. I saw the experience as an opportunity to learn.

Just remember, the important thing is to not let emotion cloud your decision-making. Stay focused.

Chapter Nine

Growing your Business – Be a Killer Competitor

Okay, you have launched your business. There are some challenges you are going to come up against. In Chapter Twelve, I will discuss advertising, marketing, and promoting your business, often for free or very cheaply. However, in this chapter, I will discuss some very important strategies that many people don't understand about becoming a killer competitor. They are strategies that are overlooked every day by business people, yet can have a huge impact on your success!

- Fight for the lowest prices – I am telling you to negotiate with your suppliers, no matter how tough it seems. They will usually have room to give discounts. Your goal should be to get the best price they offer their biggest customers. You may have to present a case that you will be a loyal customer if they help you grow your business at the outset. Maybe you can negotiate a 2% discount if you pay their invoice within seven days. Ask what it will take to get their lowest price. Every penny you can save on your "cost of goods sold" will help you to either have a lower price for your customers or allow you to increase your profits so you can grow. As nicely as possible, let your supplier know if you find out someone else is getting a better price on the same items, you will be quick to change suppliers. You cannot waste time competing with someone who is getting a better price. Getting the lowest price from your suppliers might ensure you can have lower prices than your competitors. At the very least, your prices should not be higher.

- Cut Corners – Keep all of your costs down. It doesn't sound nice, but if it can be done without any detriment to your business, then do it. For example, if you are running a restaurant and you are going to make a vegetable soup, then the vegetables don't need to look good, as they are going to be chopped up anyway. I think of this as I know a restaurant owner who pays a premium for his vegetables just because they look perfect. Why do this? Over a year, the savings can be substantial and you can meet or beat your competitors' prices.

If you have an office and need a cleaning service, do you really need a service that sends out well-dressed salespeople in nicely painted vehicles and a cleaning crew in super nice uniforms? Look for a cheaper alternative by asking others in the office building for referrals or simply get on Google. I know someone who went from paying $2,200 per month for office cleaners to $725 per month – an annual savings of $17,700. This is another $17,700 that you don't have to raise your prices to earn, meaning you might have the most competitive price for your product.

If you need cartridges for your office printers, don't buy name brands. My own office printer takes color cartridges that cost $185 each if I order from the manufacturer of my printer. I buy knock-offs from another company for $110 each. I have been doing this for at least five years and save at least $1,200 per year...over $6,000 during the last five years. Again, this is an expense that I don't have to recover in the price of my products.

As a new entrepreneur or growing small business, you must beg, borrow, and get all the free stuff you can. Don't waste your most valuable resource – Cash! Get by with spending as little as possible. Rent post office boxes, use cell phones instead of office landlines, buy your furniture at used office furniture stores, etc.

Once you have done all you can to keep costs down, you can set optimal prices for your products or services:

- Setting the Right Price – Only fools rush into pricing their goods and services. Sell on more than price – know how your products and services will enhance your customers' lives. If you are selling a gorgeous new Audi or Mercedes Benz sports car, then the right customer will not care too much about price. Sell the lifestyle.

You must know all of your costs to set the right price for your service or product. This includes the not so obvious costs such as annual property taxes, an allowance for maintenance, an allowance for legal fees, emergencies, promotional giveaways, and your share as an employer of tax withholdings.

So if you are looking at just the basic cost of what you will be selling – the price you paid your supplier – you will be out of business very quickly. In Chapter Two, I outlined some of the more specific ways to calculate all costs. Review this carefully.

I have known many friends and colleagues who opened restaurants and had working capital ranging from a few thousand dollars to several hundred thousand dollars, and in a very short period of time they lost it all. I even encouraged many of them to stop and re-price their menus or find ways to cut their costs. Instead, they made the unconscious choice to subsidize meals, for all of their customers, until they ran out of money.

Lines of people at the door does not necessarily mean success. These lines won't mean a thing if your prices don't leave you with a profit. I first learned this when I was in high school. Some poor guy opened an all-you-can-eat buffet across from the school. The lines of students, especially the football team, loved this place. Every student filled their plate at least twice and many figured out to take only the high value items. In a couple of months, he posted a sign – "No Students" – and he just magnified his troubles as now he could not allow families in because he effectively was barring children. By the time he posted a sign "Students

BUSINESS, BUSINESS, BUSINESS!

Welcome with Parents" his business was so far downhill he never recovered. So popularity can mean disaster unless you know your costs and set selling prices to ensure profit. And, choose your location wisely.

I know another friend, who along with four friends, started an Internet business. They had imported some electronics products from China and all of their inventory sold very quickly. The orders kept pouring in and more inventory was due in two weeks. Soon, they had more than $200,000 in new orders for a $25 item and they were paying the supplier $11 for the product, including shipping. Their supplier, recognizing an opportunity to squeeze their customer, raised the price to my friend to $17 and did not include the shipping. A partial order of his product was shipped Express instead of at regular rates. The new shipping expense added $4 to each item. Now there was also a charge for duty. So his cost of product was now about $22.50.

Once he had the product, he had to repackage and mail it to individual customers. With labor, packaging materials, labels, and postage, his costs were almost $27.50 to make a $25 sale – a loss of $2.50 on each item. When he called me for some ideas to solve his problem, I reminded him that all of his sales had been paid for by credit card and after a 3% commission to the credit card companies, he would be losing an additional 75 cents per sale – a total loss of $3.25 per item or $26,000 in total.

Fortunately, he had only paid the supplier for 2400 units – or $40,800. I recommended he refund ALL the customers. His arrangement with the credit card company meant he would not pay any commissions on refunded money.

I further recommended he email all customers that a refund was coming due to higher than expected manufacturing costs, but if they wished to re-order they could at a price of $34.99 and of course very few people did this.

He then offered the 2400 units on his website at a price of $34.99. It took longer to sell – about 4 weeks instead of 4 days. However, he made a profit of almost $20,000.

He had established integrity with the original customers who were made whole with the refund and now he had made a profit.

I recommended he source a new supplier on Alibaba.com and then spend $3,500 of his $20,000 profit to go to China and try to build a relationship, and document by way of a contract, the pricing at various quantities while paying only 50% as a deposit and the balance payable upon arriving at my friend's warehouse in California. He did so and has been using the same supplier for more than two years now.

In the meantime, there have been several companies that have tried to compete, but none have the competitive advantage he now enjoys.

- Dumping "Price Only" Customers – These are the worst kind of toxic customers, as they cause you to try and compete in stupid ways. Avoid them as they will eat up your time, your energy, and your money. Even if you give them the price they want to pay, they will usually be ungrateful, will complain to you anyway, and will speak poorly about you to other potential customers. Worse yet, they may tell your existing customers about the great deal they got and now you have offended a customer who paid a higher price. Unless you are running a small shop in a bazaar in Turkey

BUSINESS, BUSINESS, BUSINESS!

or a tourist trap in The Bund area of Shanghai, where haggling is expected, don't negotiate lower prices with retail customers. Maintain your profit margins. If you let these customers drag you down, your business may soon be finished.

Instead, concentrate on your profitable customers. In fact, to grow your business, you must obsess about your good customers.

- Know Your Business Type – It seems so elementary, however in my experience, many businesspeople do not think enough about what type of business they want to have as the business grows and they even end up competing with themselves. Understandably, in the early days of a startup, you might be finding your way. But once you have your footing as a new business, you must determine if you are going to be a wholesaler, a retailer, or both. If you answered both, you must then be aware of the pitfall of competing against yourself. A friend of mine made New York style bagels in Canada. He opened a café with 12 chairs and some outside seating. His fresh bagels drew crowds from afar. It was standing room only from early morning until late in the evening.

Soon, nearby coffee shops and restaurants wanted to buy bagels wholesale from my friend. He gave the coffee shops and restaurants a "volume" or wholesale discount. He provided small signs and bags so everyone would know they were his bagels. Soon, he did not have the same lines forming, as customers could get the bagels closer to their homes in the coffee shops and restaurants. Most importantly, he was losing all the revenue from the cream cheese, capers, onions, and other extras that he was selling when he made sandwich-style bagels.

The Entrepreneur's Guide to Strategies, Secrets and Savings

He was making bagels 24 hours a day when a major grocer approached and gave him an order. He thought he would just have to put two teams of bagel bakers on 24 hours a day to make the increased number of bagels. He gave it a try.

Besides all the headaches he caused himself with staff, machinery breakdowns, the purchasing of trucks and hiring of drivers, to name just a few problems, he found his revenue was way up, but his profits were almost non-existent – some months even had huge losses!

He called me up and brought his financials to me for my opinion. He was so involved in the nuts and bolts of getting enough bagels out the door seven days a week that he could not think clearly. It was easy for me to see the solution. In the past, as one small café with 12 chairs and a take-out business, he was making at least $15,000 per month for himself and in the summer months he was making more than $30,000 a month for himself – almost a quarter of a million dollars, before personal taxes, for himself and his family!

I recommended he stop selling to his wholesale clients and that he only sell from his one retail location again. This meant staff layoffs, selling his trucks (no more monthly payments, insurance, or fuel cost) and infuriating his wholesale clients.

He took my advice and within a week he was like a new man – 90% of his stress was gone, his retail business soared again, and best of all he had personal time left to enjoy his life a little more.

Is your business going to be a wholesaler, distributor, or sales rep for another company? In each case, make sure you have strong, non-compete contracts that cannot be easily

BUSINESS, BUSINESS, BUSINESS!

voided by the other side. If you are going to grow your business in one of these ways, I strongly recommend an attorney help you with the proper documentation. You don't want to do all of the hard work building a market for a manufacturer to find they don't need you and you are out in the cold. It happens all the time, so be smart as you grow your business.

- Keep an Eye on Your Vendors – There are a lot of snakes out there. You must be wary of those who might hurt you. Unfortunately, as a new business, you won't have much power over them, so you just have to take steps to protect yourself.

A couple of anecdotes to illustrate the point:

A few years ago, a 21-year-old relative of mine discovered a body cream product in England. He imported 100 bottles and sold them quickly on his new website. He ordered another 500 and they were selling quickly. He and his girlfriend were boxing each bottle in their tiny kitchen, as well as applying a label and postage for delivery. Soon, he was using his parents' home and then their garage. Finally, overwhelmed with packaging, he hired a local mailing house to take over. He dropped off cases of product and the labels were sent directly to the mailing house. New orders and re-orders came in and the business grew very quickly.

Suddenly his re-orders dropped off completely. The bank deposits were getting smaller instead of increasing. Yes, the mailing house owner had set up a relative to operate a competing business and used all of the information on the mailing labels to create a customer database for the new business. My relative's new competition then sent out an offer with a lower price. No customer loyalty, so they ordered from the new business for a lower price. The supplier would not get in the middle, saying he didn't care who he sold to. $25,000 spent on attorney's fees got my relative no satisfaction! He was furious enough he was talking about burning the man's business down, hiring someone to beat him up, and other comments made in anger.

I was able to calm him down and make some recommendations. I told him the best revenge was to get even. My relative had the original of the mailing list, so I suggested he get a complementary product from his supplier – something inexpensive – and create a bundle, the original cream and a gift that could be marketed to his customer list. So without reducing his price, but by adding a small "free" sample-size of a cream for eyelids, he won back virtually all of his customers. A few more strategies like this and the mailing house competitor soon stopped competing. Additionally, my relative rented a small building, hired his own staff, and did all the mailing himself. Then two years ago, he moved all of his sales operations to a store on Amazon.com and his life has become much simpler, and he is not concerned with Amazon competing.

In another case, a friend was excited to discover a product on Alibaba that she could re-sell on her website. Unfortunately, as her sales grew, her vendor set up his own website offering the product for 20% less. She was out of luck and shut down. The vendor simply cut her off when he saw the potential to make more money. Even if she had a contract, it would have been unenforceable in court as the supplier was overseas.

- Pricing Dynamics and Inventory Management – As a killer competitor, this is a complex topic, but let me give you an example so you can apply at least one principle of pricing dynamics to your business. If you are selling table

BUSINESS, BUSINESS, BUSINESS!

saws or lumber, there is no rush to sell your non-perishable product, so you don't need to adjust your prices too often. If you are selling fruit and vegetables, you generally have a few days to sell. If you are selling seats in a restaurant or rooms in a hotel, then you must sell them by midnight or your product is gone forever. You will never be able to sell that seat or room again.

If you are selling a service as a lawyer, accountant, dentist, chiropractor, doctor, or driving instructor, then you must sell your time every hour, and even every minute in some cases, or as soon as the day is over you will see how low your "sales" are. Of course, professionals prefer to speak of income or billable hours, but you are still selling a service and must price your time well. I have had lawyers quote me a fixed price for a project and then be ready to sit and gab with me for an extra 30 minutes...how stupid!

Once you have a good understanding of how to control costs and to set prices, you are ready to take steps to grow your business.

- Network like crazy – In this digital age, there are so many opportunities to network. It really doesn't matter what kind of business you are in – networking is very important. Trade shows, seminars, blogs, Facebook, and countless other opportunities are available. One of the most impressive networking opportunities, especially if you are working at home, is FreelancersUnion.org.

FreelancersUnion.org has 250,000 independent members and offers great resources. Two of them are:

1. FreelancersUnion Meet-up Events in cities across the country. Check out Meetup.com for details.

The Entrepreneur's Guide to Strategies, Secrets and Savings

2. Hives – "the community for the new workforce." FreelancersUnion.org describes Hives as:

"Welcome to Hives, the online community for the new workforce.

"Networks are crucial to a successful freelance life, so we wanted to build a place for independent workers to come together to connect with one another online.

"Consider it your one-stop online freelance network.

"Not sure what to charge for a gig? There's a hive for that.

"Interested in sharing your creative inspiration? There's a hive for that.

"Want to discuss the future of the economy with the people shaping it? There's a hive for that.

"But remember, Hives was your idea, so it's yours to build.

"Maybe there's something else that you'd like to talk about. Maybe you want to connect with freelancers in your city – or find solutions to common issues, like getting paid or doing your taxes. So, start a Hive and get the conversation going.

"This is a place where independent workers from across the country can come together to build the future economy. It's a place for inspiring conversations, sharing creative ideas, and working together for the benefit of all. It's about achieving meaningful independence.

"Simply, 'We're doers. We're believers. We're builders.'"

BUSINESS, BUSINESS, BUSINESS!

LinkedIn.com is clearly the outstanding choice for networking. Currently with more than 330 million members in over 200 countries, they are the network to join. Their mission is to connect the world's professionals to make them more productive and successful. Every entrepreneur should join and reap the benefits of membership.

Chamber of Commerce, Rotary, Lions Clubs – While some are more business-oriented than others, it is still a great opportunity to meet people and let them know what your business is all about. Many have opportunities for you to rent a table and present your business to others.

Industry Associations – Join your local restaurant association, homebuilders' association, or similar group that has a focus on your industry. Often these groups have negotiated better prices with suppliers or arranged discounts on insurance for your business. They generally have monthly meetings where you can learn more about what is going on in your area and the impact on your business. Many members of groups help each other. I know of several situations where homebuilders were not able to meet a prospective customer's requirements and they made a referral to another homebuilder that was worth hundreds of thousands of dollars.

Some of my best ideas for growing my businesses through networking have come from reading business oriented publications. *Forbes, Fortune, Wall Street Journal*, local business journals, and the business section of local newspapers have sparked many new ideas to promote my business.

In any event, even if reading does not give you the networking opportunity you are looking for, much other valuable information can be learned. In an issue of *Forbes* I just finished, in the section named "Top Entrepreneur,"

The Entrepreneur's Guide to Strategies, Secrets and Savings

there is a great article by George Anders on "Retail's New Power Couple." Essentially, the article details the strategies used, and values held, by Adi Tatardo and husband Alon Cohen to grow their company. Starting five years ago at their kitchen table, the couple have one of the top 200 websites in the U.S. Their site, Houzz.com, appeals to those interested in home decorating. Houzz.com draws 25 million visitors each month. The company is now valued at more than $2 billion.

This article is typical of what I mean when I say that some of my best ideas for growing a company come from reading *Forbes* and other business publications.

• Watch Your Competition – Hopefully you have an original idea and you won't have any competition! Hah! However, even if you discover such an idea, you will soon have lots of competition if your idea is any good. Depending upon your level of sophistication, you may be able to monitor the competition and adjust your prices accordingly. But never have the highest prices, no matter how great you think you are. You just don't have a brand as strong as Tiffany or Neiman Marcus to pull it off! The public – your customers – will just not buy from you for long. The vast majority of customers are very price sensitive.

Look at Frontier Airlines, Southwest Airlines, and Allegiant Air in America, or Ryanair and easyJet in Europe. Their flights have the cheapest fares, are usually packed, and they charge you for every possible thing. Most people are willing to put up with a lack of comfort to save money.

People just don't care about your business if your prices are too high. I know of a corner in my hometown with three restaurants on three of the corners. At two of the restaurants, you can get eggs and coffee for $7.25 and they are both packed from 6 a.m. to 3 p.m. when they close. The

BUSINESS, BUSINESS, BUSINESS!

third charges $7.95 and has few customers at any time of the day. The third has terrible servers as well, since the restaurant does not create an environment where they can earn any tips.

If your business allows you to create a dynamic pricing model, then that is optimal. Hotels and airlines have revenue managers who work full-time monitoring their competitors' pricing and either setting higher prices or lowering prices to ensure their hotel rates and airline fares reflect a fair deal while driving business in the door.

- Wage War on Your Competition – Dominate your market in order to grow! Make sure you are offering a superior product or service supported by outstanding customer service to do this. You are in a war as you grow your company and must fight for your customers. For new entrepreneurs, there is truth in the proven adage: Focus on your repeat customers and getting referrals.

In my businesses, I have become more aggressive with the use of the Internet to gather market intelligence about my competitors. In this digital age, the reputation of your business is online for the world to see. This is the era of customer power! Your customers can make or ruin you with their online comments. If you sell your product on Amazon.com, then you know very well that a good reputation will generate referral business. With a great online reputation, you let others sell for you, giving you time to grow your business. If you are a plumber in Kansas City, or an electrician anywhere in the U.S.A., you know the power of Yelp.com. Great reviews mean new business. Poor reviews and you might as well close up shop!

Restaurants and hotels live or die by their reviews on OpenTable.com and TripAdvisor.com.

The Entrepreneur's Guide to Strategies, Secrets and Savings

So to wage war on your competitors, you need to know what they are doing – something called market intelligence. Go to the various review sites that might apply to your business and check for your competitors' weaknesses and strengths and learn how to improve your business to satisfy customers' needs even better.

I use a great tool – Google Alerts. Sign up for Google Alerts at google.com/alerts and put in your competitors' information. You will then be alerted by Google anytime anything appears on the Internet about your competitors. It may be as simple as seeing that one of your competitors is hiring a new General Manager. Why? Has your restaurant competitor hired three new chefs in three months? Is there a weakness you can exploit?

Google Alerts will notify you when a competitor issues a press release about a new product or service.

You should also enter your information so you can monitor what is being said about your business on the Internet.

I follow my competitors on their Facebook pages for announcements. Should you be doing the same? They might be putting on special events that draw customers in. Do you know about these special events? Should you be planning a special event?

If you are selling products on the web, then you should be using the same tactics to learn about your competitors as brick-and-mortar retailers do.

Monitor the Twitter, Pinterest, and Instagram accounts of your competitors. You have to know what they are doing in order to wage war and grow your market share.

BUSINESS, BUSINESS, BUSINESS!

If you are in retail, hire a mystery shopper who will go into your competitor's store and find out what they are selling and who their suppliers are. The big retailers all do this type of espionage.

If you are running a restaurant, ask a relative or friend to sit outside your competitor's restaurant for a couple of mornings and have them write down the names on the delivery trucks. Call those suppliers and check on what they have to sell and especially their prices and any special offers.

- Solve Pain Points in the Marketplace – A pain point generally represents an opportunity for an entrepreneur and therefore an opportunity to grow your business.

Kristen Carsen, President of Freshman Support and Contributing Writer for *Texas Enterprise,* of The University of Texas at Austin, wrote a great article on the subject. An excerpt:

"You can trace most successful companies' beginnings to the basic objective of solving a pain point in the marketplace. A few examples:

"Google provided a search engine that allowed people to find websites and explore the Internet without knowing the URL of every page.

"Netflix saved people the trouble of going to a video store and worrying about late fees.

"Apple provided a computer that an average person could employ for personal use (and later introduced a device that could store and play hundreds of songs in your pocket).

"Why is solving a problem so important? There are two main benefits to solving a problem: 1) Your product will be

The Entrepreneur's Guide to Strategies, Secrets and Savings

much easier to market, and 2) you can more easily measure the market potential, which makes it easier to value your company for investors, better to understand pricing, and easier to test your product because you know who your market is."

- Focus on Your Core Products or Services – A big mistake that entrepreneurs make when trying to compete is losing focus and trying to be all things to all customers. If you have a great product and it is selling well, then don't be foolish and add a product that is completely unrelated, especially when you are just starting out. Nothing will put off your investors, lenders, and especially your customers more than if your business does not make sense.

In France, I met a man and woman who had a cute little restaurant. But once I sat down, I realized they had taken down a wall and put a line of washers and dryers along the far wall. I noticed a woman folding her underwear at the end of the building. It just put me off to think of people bringing in their dirty laundry to a place where I was planning on eating. I got up and left, wondering what these owners were thinking.

In my gym, which is actually called a wellness center, they have a café set up for members and staff. In five years, I don't think I have seen more than two or three people eating anything there, yet every day I see sandwich making ingredients, sodas, potato chips, and desserts for sale. While they claim to be healthy choices, it seems to me that people that have come to the building to work out and presumably lose weight are not going to spend much time in a café. Sure a smoothie bar might work, but a whole selection of food items? I am sure it is a losing venture, yet management will tell you that the budget is tight and they cannot add instructors for more classes! Craziness!

BUSINESS, BUSINESS, BUSINESS!

Don't add lines of products that will compete for your customers' dollars. If you are selling a good line of soaps and making money, don't sell towels, even if it seems to make sense. If a customer is on your website or in your store, sell them soap. They probably came in with an amount they were going to spend on soap. Let them go somewhere else to buy towels. Besides, no one returns soap, but people do return towels for many reasons and each return will hurt your profits.

Chapter Ten

Without Sales, Nothing Else Matters

Now that you have given your pricing and costing strategies plenty of thought, you must consider those sales and other management issues that will arise as you grow. In my experience, these are the key strategies that you must implement as you manage growth.

- Automate – Use software whenever possible, so sales management should be your focus. By this stage of your growth, you have your accounting systems as automated as possible.

Most businesses will need an automated method of identifying and servicing customers to manage their growth. I still meet entrepreneurs who are carrying a wad of business cards from their customers wrapped in an elastic band. This is insane! Today, free apps are available for your smartphone that allow you to scan a business card and it will automatically be added to your contacts.

I have used and can recommend two amazing customer relationship managers (CRMs) that offer so much for a relatively low cost. Deciding which program to choose will depend on how you visualize the growth of your company.

The first company is called PipelineDeals.com and I recommend it for companies wanting a simple method of managing customer relationships and sales. The simplicity is great for companies who want their salespeople making calls and not filling in on-screen forms and reports. Management can log on anytime and view the activity of the sales team. It also works well for many companies as there is no contract and you can pay monthly. The price is $24 per month, per user. And, there is no software to update.

Some of the key features excerpted from the website of PipelineDeals.com:

BUSINESS, BUSINESS, BUSINESS!

"We designed PipelineDeals to make you and your team more productive. Our features deliver plenty of power to manage your sales process and learn from your data, but they never waste your time with unnecessary complexity.

"Receive a daily pipeline snapshot – Every day PipelineDeals sends the Morning Coffee Report to your email inbox. This report provides an overview of the prior day's progress and your latest sales pipeline numbers. It's a great way to stay current and identify trends.

"Manage everything about a deal in one place – Each deal you add in PipelineDeals gets its own comprehensive page. With 12 standard data fields and up to 25 custom fields, you can track as much detail as you like. Deal pages also consolidate all activities, people, documents, tasks, and events."

- View real-time deal status updates – From your PipelineDeals home page, you can see all the latest activity on your deals. Managers can see activity on all their team deals, and executives can see all deal activity company-wide. Click on any item to go directly to the deal page and get more information.

Even if you do nothing more than record the company name, contact name, phone number, and a brief note about the phone call or visit, you will find the benefits of being organized well worth the monthly fee.

Now if you consider yourself extremely computer savvy and believe you can use a comprehensive customer relationship program, then Salesforce.com offers the best there is in my opinion. I have used this service with large sales teams and the information and reports are amazing. But naturally it comes at a price. While prices start at $25 per user, per month for up to five users, the cost can rise as high as $250

The Entrepreneur's Guide to Strategies, Secrets and Savings

per user, per month for unlimited use and support for your whole team – and it is an annual commitment. If your company has grown considerably, then Salesforce.com is for you.

Some of the key features excerpted from the website of Salesforce.com:

"Close more deals – No matter the size of your company, all sales reps share one common goal — the desire to be a top performer. We can help with that.

"Contact Management – Have a complete view of your customers, including activity history, key contacts, customer communications, and internal account discussions. Gain insights from popular social media sites such as Facebook, Twitter, LinkedIn, and YouTube — right within Salesforce.

"Opportunity Management – Get all the details on your team's deals — stage, products, competition, quotes, and more. Stay connected to the people and information you need to close every sale.

"Sales Collaboration – Tap into the wisdom of your company's social network with Chatter. Get the resources you need to close more deals, faster. Find experts, access competitive information, and track deals wherever you are.

"Sales Performance Management – Drive team performance to a whole new level with Work.com. Set metrics-based goals, give coaching notes, provide continuous feedback, and amplify winning behaviors with real-time recognition and rewards.

"Lead Management – Make smarter decisions about where to invest your marketing dollars. Track your leads

BUSINESS, BUSINESS, BUSINESS!

from click to close, while continually optimizing your campaigns across every channel.

"*Marketing Automation – Create, deploy, and manage effective online campaigns with Pardot Marketing Automation. Now your sales and marketing teams can work hand-in-hand to generate and qualify leads, shorten sales cycles, and demonstrate marketing accountability.*"

Again, it is all about you making the right decision for your company, but it is essential to automate your sales management process as you grow.

- Don't Get Committed to Costs – As you grow, you must still be nervous about taking on fixed costs. In my early business days, I made a lot of mistakes by taking on costs that had to be paid regardless of my sales, especially staffing costs. In my personnel business, I hired "personnel counselors" whose job it was to interview and send staff to hotels. I had negotiated contracts with many hotels and logging and mining camps in Alaska and northern Canada where it was really hard to find and keep employees. These hotels and camps contracted with me to find employees in the U.S. and Canada and then fly them to the jobs. I received a fee for each employee I sent. My personnel counselors worked with the hotels to meet their specific needs and take care of airline tickets and other details. Things were going so well that I signed a lease for office space, for five years, and also leased vehicles to take these new employees to the airport. I even entered contracts with newspapers to do a minimum amount of advertising each year. My ads in the Yellow Pages were sizeable and non-cancellable.

However, about a year later, the economy tanked and none of my clients wanted to hire more staff. I laid off most of the personnel counselors (ironically they had demanded greater commissions a month earlier). However, I still had monthly payments for office space, leased vehicles, newspaper advertising, and my Yellow Page ads.

Fortunately, I came up with another business idea and used the office space, got friends to take over the car lease payments, and advertised my new business in the newspaper. Only Yellow Pages refused to work with me and so I obtained a new phone number for the new business and Yellow Pages went away.

Avoid cost commitments if at all possible. If you need more staff, try to hire part-time people, independent contractors, or even see if your family and friends can help out until you are 100% sure you are ready to hire full-time personnel.

- Hire a Great Management Team – As you grow your company, there will be nothing more important than a great management team, especially those responsible for sales. It is time for you as a startup entrepreneur to begin to delegate responsibilities to others. Expect this to be tough. Most often, entrepreneurs are terrible administrators or managers, so your first step should be to find someone you feel comfortable working with that will be very good at taking care of the operational details. You should be focusing on opportunities to take revenue to the next level. Depending on the type of business you are growing, you most likely will need someone to handle production, someone to handle hiring, and someone to handle deliveries. This team will complement the bookkeeper or accountant that has been with you since the startup days. You should evaluate the skill level of your accountant and you may have to replace him or her with a more skilled person. Your numbers are only going to get bigger and systems will need to be designed to handle the more sophisticated aspects of a growing business.

BUSINESS, BUSINESS, BUSINESS!

- Time Management Impacts Sales Performance – Again, you will have to learn how to delegate to allow yourself time to focus on sales and growth. Operational staff meetings should be at a minimum, and when you do have meetings, create an agenda first so the meetings don't drag on. Ideally, you will only discuss matters that can be supported by data – matters such as filling orders, staffing needs, and cash flow requirements. Encourage feedback; otherwise, this will just be a meeting where everyone agrees with you because it is the boss speaking.

As the president of one of my companies long ago, I was the typical boss who thought he knew it all and the staff loved and respected me. I always got positive feedback about what a great boss I was. One day, I read about a company that would come to my office and conduct a "real" evaluation of what staff thought of me.

A man from that company came out and in our meeting room he set up a big divider that was impossible to see through. He then asked me to go on one side and my staff on the other. He had a device that scrambled my employees' voices and he led them through a number of business issues.

I was flabbergasted at what my employees were saying about me – first, my time management was terrible, my fairness to them, their projects, lack of recognition, meetings I conducted, their pay, their benefits, their vacations, the equipment in the office, and their workspaces were all lacking. The truth really came out. I was making notes and I am glad to say that within three months, it was a whole new company – really enthusiastic team, much higher sales, and a new respect among all of us. The changes I made in my personnel management style have stayed with me the rest of my life.

The Entrepreneur's Guide to Strategies, Secrets and Savings

Today, we have some valuable tools that we can use to improve our business lives. I use my calendar on my computer to set important events only. Then if it is not on my calendar, I don't do it. Of course, my calendar is synced with my smartphone and tablet I carry everywhere.

In the interest of good time management, I avoid phone calls unless they are from clients or family. All others can text or email me. I prefer emails because it is so easy to set up a folder for someone's emails, or by project, and then I have a full record. I am sure almost everyone is doing this, so if you are not, it is a good time to start.

- Pick your challenges – You have to learn to get rid of toxic people in your business life. Time is money and you will find you must be rude once in a while if you are going to have time for sales development. I had a supplier once who had a great final product, but every detail of production was a hassle. Even when the price was agreed upon in writing, he would try to boost the price as delivery day got closer. Every time he came into my office, I knew there was going to be a problem. After 30 minutes of him saying nothing but nonsense, I looked at him and said, "Please leave my office. I am taking my business elsewhere. Don't say another word." Stunned, he turned and left. I quickly found another supplier who met my needs.

In the past, I have had large entities as customers who drove me crazy with their demands. In my publishing business, a large public utility invited us to bid on doing all of their printing of publications. I believed this would be good for our reputation and our bottom line. However, after 19 meetings with various people and committees to discuss ideas, and where I was always expected to bring samples and PowerPoint presentations, I told them I was no longer interested in their work. My contacts got angry with me and made all sorts of threats. However, my costs were quickly adding up and a decision by them seemed months away. I have never regretted pulling away from this challenge.

I have usually found that sales to governments and major organizations like utilities are just not worth the trouble in the end for a small company. The paperwork alone is unbelievable. However, the business can provide a boost at times and if you have the patience, it can certainly be profitable. The federal government, through the Small Business Administration, is always attempting to make selling to the government easier. I think just by the nature and size of the organization you are dealing with that it will never be easy. If you are interested in this kind of business, check out the Business Matchmaking Program sponsored by the U.S. Chamber of Commerce and the SBA. The program is intended to match entrepreneurs with government contracts.

Additionally, I have learned that when a great salesperson starts to cause me grief, I just fire them; otherwise, they impact sales. There was a time in the early days when I would show empathy, try to understand their personal issues, and pay them even when their work was substandard. Without fail, every effort at helping was a waste of my time and money. I hope every new entrepreneur learns this lesson faster than I did. Now if you have time to help others in your personal life, that is a different matter.

- Scalable Business Growth – There is some confusion over the use of the business jargon "a scalable business." If seen from an investor's point of view, a business with scalable growth means the business has the potential to multiply revenues with a minimum of increased cost. This

The Entrepreneur's Guide to Strategies, Secrets and Savings

applies almost entirely to Internet businesses and is a major topic best discussed at another time.

For most entrepreneurs growing their business, a scalable business means being able to meet sudden increased sales demand. For example, if your business sells a really unique t-shirt for a particular event and it is sold on your website, are you ready for 10,000 orders? Is your online transaction processing set up to handle a huge volume? Is your server for your website ready for increased volume? Can you create 10,000 t-shirts quickly? Can you ship 10,000 t-shirts quickly?

Maybe with some planning, a t-shirt company can scale up quickly. However, a florist probably could not.

The orders might not be online. Would you be able to manage the growth if a major grocery chain, or other big box store, wanted 50,000 units of your product when you generally sell 10,000 units a year?

So before you dream too big, ask yourself is my business truly scalable if sales increase greatly?

- Opening Another Location – This road to more sales appeals to many entrepreneurs with a retail business. Usually, it is a bad idea. First, you have to ask yourself if your existing location is maximizing all the sales possible. Then you will have to consider the following issues:

—Does your business have a proven track record of sales and profitability over several years?

—Do you personally have the energy to travel to more than one location a day, if necessary?

—Is your management team optimized?

BUSINESS, BUSINESS, BUSINESS!

—Do you have the processes and systems in place to handle another location?

—Have you done a SWOP analysis for the new location?

—Do you have a location in mind that is based on what is best for the business and not what suits you best?

—If you are thinking partnership for the new locations, do you have an experienced attorney and accountant who can assist you to navigate the expansion?

- Be Open to New Ideas for Generating Sales – Alipay is a service for U.S. companies who want to sell their products to China's 500 million online shoppers who spent $298 billion online in 2013. The service is called EPass and is available to any U.S. retailer interested in reaching the Chinese consumer. Alipay targets English-reading young professionals in the four biggest regions of China. EPass aims to make purchasing American products easier. Chinese shoppers will pay in yuan and merchants can be paid in U.S. dollars, among other currencies. Visit global.alipay.com for more information.

- Are you ready to be committed to growing your business? Ask yourself the hardest possible questions. For example: If I create and really promote my web business, and I am incredibly successful, am I ready to live in China if necessary to keep products coming to meet demand? I have known people who have moved to China, and I have known others who said no way, because of family obligations at home. There is no point in planning to grow a super successful website if you are not ready to make really difficult choices. The same question applies to all types of businesses. To increase sales in my fishing business, and to keep supply coming, I found myself on fishing boats, on rough ocean waves, wondering if I was ever going to see land

The Entrepreneur's Guide to Strategies, Secrets and Savings

or my family again. Learning to fire burned out salespeople was also very tough. Talk is easy, but looking someone in the eyes and telling them they are no longer needed was very difficult at first.

- Always Keep Learning. To drive sales and the growth of your business in any industry, you will find the industry is constantly changing and you must be ready to keep up, or better yet, be a leader. This may mean traveling to trade shows, networking constantly, attending continuing education opportunities, reading extensively, and researching on websites that are relevant to your business.

- Team Participation. Give your team, from the bottom up, a chance to participate and benefit from the growth of your company. For example, if you are getting new sales leads, make sure your existing sales team gets as many as they can handle before hiring anyone new. If you have a retail shop, incentivize the clerks so they have a reason to sell more, as a minimum wage is not going to motivate anyone to do extra.

In my offices, I always had a policy that if I got a call or letter or email from someone complimenting our receptionist, then I would give her an extra $10 bonus for each compliment in that month. She also knew if I found out she asked someone for a compliment that she would get nothing for three months.

She was inspired to smile and treat everyone, in person or on the phone, like they were the most important person to our business. Most months, she received at least $100 extra.

As you can see, managing the sales and growth of your business has many factors to consider; however, if you are ready for the challenge, then you are in for some really exciting and rewarding times!

Chapter Eleven

Design, Prototypes, and Contract Manufacturing

To allow your business to grow, you must think bigger all the time. For example, if you are making and packaging your product at home or in a small facility, you must think about a more professional and automated process to grow. Cutting per unit costs while increasing supply to meet demand is key to your growth. This is often accomplished by using a Contract Manufacturer or CM. In the food business, this company is usually called a co-packer.

Wikipedia defines a Contract Manufacturing business relationship as:

"In a contract manufacturing business model, the hiring firm approaches the contract manufacturer with a design or formula. The contract manufacturer will quote the parts based on processes, labor, tooling, and material costs. Typically a hiring firm will request quotes from multiple CMs. After the bidding process is complete, the hiring firm will select a source, and then, for the agreed-upon price, the CM acts as the hiring firm's factory, producing and shipping units of the design on behalf of the hiring firm."

Contract Manufacturers offer a wide range of facilities – commercial kitchens; food packaging; general and rapid prototyping; machining; fabricating with welders, laser cutters, and water jet cutting; painting; engineering; assembling and inspecting.

Just a few of the products that can be contract manufactured for you include:

- Aluminum bottles
- Appliances
- Baby/Children products
- Cable assemblies
- Computer products

BUSINESS, BUSINESS, BUSINESS!

- Electronic products
- Food service equipment
- Gifts
- Hardware
- Home products
- LED products
- Medical products
- Packaging equipment
- Replicas
- Security products
- Solar energy products
- Springs
- Telecommunication products
- Tubing

Thomasnet.com is my favorite source to go to when I am in need of a contract manufacturer. When I last checked, this valuable resource listed 5,163 contract manufacturers. You can search with many filters so that you can find a company near to you, companies that are owned by minorities, women, or veterans and you can even filter by special certifications you many want, such as ISO 9000, ISO 9001, ISO 9002, and others. If you are considering ISO certification, then you will want to find an expert, as this is too complex a topic for most people to understand fully. However, with certain products, it gives buyers assurance that your product meets advanced standards.

Benefits of contract manufacturing include:

- Cost savings – You don't need to invest in equipment and a physical plant.

- Advanced skills availability – You can leave the engineering, fabricating, and production to someone else.

- Quality – You can specify a certain level of materials and quality in your contract.

- Focus – You can focus on your core competency, such as sales, and leave production to others.

- Economies of scale – Often your contract manufacturer can obtain supplies for a lower cost than you can. Think of a large contract baker who makes bread, cookies, cupcakes, and other pastries for many customers. The baker's cost of flour and other ingredients is certain to be less than if you bought them for your smaller business.

However, there are risks associated with contract manufacturers:

- Lack of control – When you turn your production process over to someone else, you are agreeing to allow them to do it their way while following your instructions in a written agreement. Maybe they will use a different flour in the baking process. Maybe they will use a different plastic to make your toys. Maybe their idea of red for your packaging will be different than you expected. If a specific color is important to you, then specify a Pantone color of red. The more specific you are about every detail, the better the final result.

- Relationships – Your contract manufacturer produces goods for many clients. How will you get the service you need and want? Will they take care of customers with bigger orders first? Try to create a positive and profitable relationship and most of all pay as agreed or even before.

- IP or Intellectual Property loss – If you have a component to your product that is proprietary (you invented it) and you don't want others to know the details, you must take steps to protect your information. If your contract manufacturer is low on integrity, he may try to copy your idea and sell it himself. Most contract manufacturers value their reputation far too much, but even a rogue employee might download your drawings for that unique electronic component and try to sell it to a competitor. If your propriety information is that unique, you have probably had a lawyer protect it for you and you should have the same lawyer protect you with the contract manufacturer. This is usually done with indemnity agreements, insurance policies, and financial penalties.

- Long lead times – You can't just produce another 10,000 items with your contract manufacturer to meet sudden demand. You must make arrangements with your contract manufacturer and possibly wait until they can accommodate you. This can be a major problem if your manufacturer is overseas, if for no other reason than your product may be on a boat for two weeks.

- Loss of flexibility – You will not be able to easily respond to customer requirements. Your customer may have ordered 30,000 units of your electronic device. However, for the next order of 50,000 units, what do you do if they want a variety of colors and sizes? If you have your own facility, you might be able to start production immediately and meet the order. Your contract manufacturer may not be able to meet your needs. However, this is probably not a good enough reason for you to buy a building, equipment, and materials in your early growth phase, just in case this is your last order from your customer. The strategy is to have more than one contract manufacturer who can meet your needs standing by as Plan B.

If you do decide to outsource to a contract manufacturer, there are two good sources of sample contracts that I like to use – contracts.onecle.com and intracen.org. Both sites

The Entrepreneur's Guide to Strategies, Secrets and Savings

offer sample agreements and best of all they are free. The first is for simple domestic agreements and the second is for more complex international agreements.

In any event, if you are creating an agreement with a contract manufacturer, even if they supply the agreement, the following elements should be included:

- Order number
- Names and addresses of parties
- Purpose of agreement
- Items to be manufactured with full description and materials to be used
- Quantity to be produced
- Unit price
- Total price
- Product quality standard (be specific such as "free from defects in design, workmanship, and materials")
- Title/Risk of loss (should cover possible delivery issues – make manufacturer responsible until product is received by you)
- IP and trademarks ownership
- Confidentiality (they should not say they are manufacturing for you – let your customer think you are doing your own manufacturing)
- Cooperation and improvements (what if the manufacturer has an idea to make your product better – at least get a change order in writing)
- Duration of agreement
- Force Majeure (deals with non-performance for reasons such as war, fire, earthquake)
- Hardship (deals with financial troubles, labor disputes)
- No partnership or agency

BUSINESS, BUSINESS, BUSINESS!

- Assignment and subcontracting (this was a recent issue for Wal-Mart and other companies who thought they were dealing with an approved manufacturer, but in fact the manufacturer subcontracted to a company with sub-standard working conditions)
- Payment terms
- Delivery date
- Dispute resolution
- Applicable law covering agreement (make it an American court that has jurisdiction – International dispute resolution processes exist, but stay away from these as they can be very expensive)
- Termination and consequences

As you can see, it would probably be a good idea to use an attorney to draft these agreements if the amount of money is significant to you and the product has proprietary aspects, such as those found in electronic devices.

On the other hand, if it is a small amount of money for some baked items, then a handshake might be good enough. An attorney would be overkill in this situation.

Chapter Twelve

Free or Cheap Marketing and Branding

As entrepreneurs, we are very fortunate to live in a time when there are so many opportunities to grow a business at a very low cost.

There is a very important business concept you will hear about called "customer acquisition cost." Simply put, this means the amount you have to spend to get a new customer. You make this calculation by adding up all the money you spend on advertising and promotion in a defined period and then adding up the number of new customers you have. You divide the cost by the number of new customers and you will get a dollar figure known as your customer acquisition cost. Any investor will want to know this precise number and to see that the cost is dropping over time.

So the goal is to get as many customers as possible at the lowest possible cost.

Since there are so many different businesses starting up, I am going to list all of the ideas I have used over the years and let you, the reader, choose the ideas you think will work best for your business.

These ideas are for new entrepreneurs and growing businesses with limited funds. If you can afford to hire a public relations firm and advertising agency, then you probably don't need to read any further in this chapter.

- Business Cards – These are often unnecessary these days. Spend money on business cards only if you have a real need and then use a company like Vistaprint.com. They offer 100 cards for $15 or 500 for $25 – as little as five cents each. If you Google "free business cards," Vistaprint and others often offer some basic cards for free in the hope of getting your future business.

BUSINESS, BUSINESS, BUSINESS!

- Signage – If you operate your business from a retail location, then you will need a sign. Be careful not to get carried away with an expensive sign. Many companies will want to lease or sell you an expensive sign. You must consider what type of location you have. If your store is in a mall, then they will have their own rules and regulations about types of signage.

However, if you have a free-standing building, it will be important to have an effective sign – one that has your logo and name in large lettering so it can be seen clearly from a distance and someone can determine what you are offering. Do not clutter your sign with hours, phone number, and website URL. People driving by won't have time to read it. Pedestrians can just come in and ask questions.

Just keep cost in mind. You can always buy a better sign in the future if your business is doing well. Make sure the sign is done by a professional to convey the best image for your business. Sign painters have less expensive options like painting on corrugated plastic or plywood. When designing your sign, think about what is important to you as you drive by signs of other businesses.

- Handwritten Thank You Cards – A very inexpensive way for many businesses to acknowledge their appreciation for a client's business. I recently received a thank you card from a bank where I just opened an account, signed by the manager who enclosed her business card. My chiropractor sends out thank you cards to new patients. It is a nice touch by local small businesses that helps to build loyalty.

Another personal touch that customers appreciate is when they are personally thanked for their business as they are leaving the store or restaurant. This is remembered by many customers.

The Entrepreneur's Guide to Strategies, Secrets and Savings

- Speeches and Presentations – A terrific and free way for many professionals to build a client base. Accountants can offer to speak to business groups, at senior citizen homes, and to college business clubs. Chiropractors and medical doctors can talk on relevant topics at health clubs, wellness centers, and sports groups such as running clubs and ski clubs. All it takes is a phone call to introduce yourself and then speak on a topic that will be of interest. In any case, remember to bring business cards or a flyer that you can leave to promote your service.

- Press Releases – I have always found that press releases are a very effective way to get your message to a large number of people. There are many companies that offer a distribution service and I have found PRWeb.com to be the best. A few words from their website:

"PRWeb is one of the easiest ways to boost your visibility online because we use search engine-friendly releases. You can include images, videos and attachments in your PRWeb releases, which can make it easier for prospects and customers to find your content online. Distribution is to more than 250,000 subscribers and as many as 30,000 bloggers and journalists."

They have excellent consultants ready to help you put together a press release and within hours your information might be found on Google, Yahoo, and Bing search engines. And, your information will remain in many places on the Internet for years to come.

Their rates start at $99 for one press release and of course more options are available. There are also many sites offering free press release distribution. Just Google "free press release distribution."

BUSINESS, BUSINESS, BUSINESS!

- Parking Lot Flyers – Personally I hate it when I find one of these on my windshield, but if you are an entrepreneur with a small shop, pizza place, or hairdressing salon, I know people in all of these fields who have had great success. A local printer can design and print plenty of these on bright colored paper for very little cost.

- Door Hangers – Not as irritating to me as parking lot flyers, but a close second. Again, I have recommended these to clients. I know several businesses that get great results. My dry cleaner says they have built his business. These bright cards are put on every door in your business territory for people to find when they get home. I like a company called CheapDoorHangers.com with prices starting at $29 per thousand when you order 5,000. There are many companies, possibly with better prices, so just Google "Door Hangers" and your location.

- Postcards – Postcards can be printed by companies like CheapDoorHangers.com that can then be delivered by the U.S. Postal Service to homes in your trading area. Or, there is probably a company in your area that can take care of all the design, printing, and distribution for you at a reasonable price. Shop around as prices can vary greatly.

- Punch Cards – This is a method of creating loyalty. Many coffee shops, car washes, and other small businesses use these cards to track your purchases. Once you reach 10 purchases, you have earned a free coffee or car wash. The cards are cheap to create and keep customers coming back. Would these work for your business?

- Banners – There are large banners, called feather and teardrop banners, that you can temporarily put in front of your business to draw attention. Unfortunately, there are often local laws prohibiting these banners; however, many

The Entrepreneur's Guide to Strategies, Secrets and Savings

businesses choose to use them until told otherwise. Prices start at $49 and go on up depending on quality and quantity. I have been told that BuildaSign.com is a reliable company to use. Or, just Google "feather and teardrop banners" and the name of your city or town.

- Car and Truck Signage – These, or even full vehicle wraps, can get attention in your neighborhood. Often, vans and trucks will have an additional sign asking passersby to take a magnetic business card off the side of the vehicle. I know screen repair services, plumbers, electricians, and others who are parked at a customer's house who use these magnetic business cards so that neighbors may call when these services are needed.

An interesting twist on this concept is to put your ads on trucks or vehicles that go where your customers are. In my area, there is a food service truck called Monika's that travels to construction sites and feeds construction workers. On each truck there are several signs from Pike Insurance offering insurance for contractors. What a great idea and at little cost!

There are also flatbed trucks that will have large signs put on the back and they spend all day driving around a certain territory. These signs are seen by thousands of people every day.

- Referral Programs – Simple cards on a store counter or emails offering a free month if you refer a friend who buys your product. Health clubs often use this form of promotion.

- Cross-promotion – Offer a fellow merchant, maybe a pet store, to set up a small display in your gift shop if they will agree to let you set up a small display in their store. They don't have to be similar businesses. A bank in my neighborhood does this for its business customers. One week

BUSINESS, BUSINESS, BUSINESS!

an art gallery has a display and another week it is a car detailing company on display. The bank changes the display often and it is right by the main entrance, which gives lots of exposure to each business.

- Email Marketing – Although I detest getting so many emails from companies that I have no intention of doing business with, I do like to get emails with special offers from businesses that I patronize. I buy special organic products from a company. The company asked me to put my email address in a book on their counter to learn of special offers. I receive a monthly email and often place an order based on needing the products and the price being a good deal.

For my own companies, I use email as a way to keep in touch and to develop new business. One of my businesses provides a service to hotels worldwide. We are constantly adding emails and then marketing to those companies. We also try to follow-up with an email on a general topic of interest to our clients.

We use ConstantContact.com and have for more than five years. I have tried other email management firms; however, ConstantContact.com is the easiest and best value in my opinion. Plans start at $15 for up to 500 contacts. Even if you have 10,000 contacts, the cost is still $85 month. You can get a 60-day free trial and there are no long-term obligations.

They offer custom templates with drag and drop editing. You can build your lists with their help by pulling email addresses from your Facebook page, company website, or even with a "text to join" program.

Other ConstantContact.com services and features include:

The Entrepreneur's Guide to Strategies, Secrets and Savings

Contact Management – stores contacts and even allows you to segment lists for different purposes

Mobile Friendly – templates are available so your emails will be seen on smartphones and tablets

Image and file storage – build a library of images for use in your emails

Social Media – integrate your email campaign with a social media toolkit

Track Activity – you will have access to a dashboard that will tell you how many of your emails were sent out, how many were deleted without being read, and "bounces," which indicate dead email addresses

Support – I have found ConstantContact.com's support to be outstanding. They are easy to reach and understand by phone. They even conduct training seminars in many areas to ensure you are maximizing the benefits of their service.

As you develop your business, and your level of sophistication grows, there are other companies that offer unbelievable customer communication tools. Two of these that I like are Hubspot.com and Marketo.com. Their much higher rates reflect the tools they offer. However, as a new or smaller entrepreneur, I encourage you to conserve your cash and start with an inexpensive service like that of ConstantContact.com.

In any event, make your email content fun and valuable to receive. Make people want to open your emails. You will often hear that content is king and no other statement could be truer with Internet-based marketing. If you have a personal relationship with a client or patient, as a chiropractor does, then maybe tell a story about your family – a new birth, a new pet, a vacation, a bike ride for charity, etc.

BUSINESS, BUSINESS, BUSINESS!

An attorney might email his business clients about an important change in law, new information on changes to the minimum wage, new dates for filing documents with government agencies, or perhaps a local story about someone going to jail for hiring illegal immigrants. Just make the content interesting and valuable.

A nursery might talk about how the owner has traveled great distances to find new and unique plants. Add photos of course. Or does the nursery offer any seminars? That is a great, almost free way to build loyalty. Have a book at the check-out area for customers to enter their email address. Perhaps have a drawing for a prize for each person who enters their email address.

A fishing lodge can market several months ahead of fishing season with photos of big fish being landed last year, current photos of the boats being painted for the next season, and changes such as a hot tub being added at the fishing lodge. Insert a link back to your YouTube channel.

- YouTube Channel – As your business grows, consider a YouTube channel where you can upload videos about your business. There is no cost other than your time. YouTube offers strategies to build your fan base, also at no cost. Start at Youtube.com.

Chapter Thirteen

Social Media and Marketing Your Business

Facebook – No one can deny Facebook's positive impact on a growing business. Can you think of a better way to be in front of almost every customer in your market area?

As an entrepreneur, there are a few key points for you to know about Facebook and what it can mean for your business.

My apologies to those who know the following. However, there are many new entrepreneurs who need to learn the basics.

Virtually every kind of business needs a Facebook account and it is FREE, unless you choose to spend money on advertising.

This is very important to know – when you open a business account, you will be assigned a strange looking name with the word 'pages' and lots of numbers in the URL. A URL is what you enter to do a search.

This is an example of a very awkward URL: https://www.facebook.com/pages/Tiger-Striped-Cats/ 107291992644945

As you build your Facebook page, ask your friends and families to 'Like' your page at your URL that looks like the one above.

Once you have 25 Likes to your page, you can change your name to a cleaner, easier to read and remember URL.

For example: facebook.com/CaliforniaStateParks

As most people know, you do not need to type "https://www." into search engines any longer.

Adding photos and videos to your Facebook page is easy after you have done it once. The important thing again is

BUSINESS, BUSINESS, BUSINESS!

the content you add to your Facebook page on a regular basis. The same fun, informative content that you put into your emails is a good starting point for your Facebook postings. Very quickly though, you will have to learn how to create content that engages those who receive your Facebook feed. If you are operating a restaurant, then try posting photos of a meal that has been created for a special occasion. Or let your followers know about any community involvement of your business. This information is then sent to those who have Liked you – hopefully your customers.

The benefit to your customers Liking you is that you will send them fun, useful content including information on special discounts. Hotels often offer special Facebook rates. Florists offer special pricing on certain floral arrangements. Just use your imagination. But do it often. One of my favorite Facebook pages to follow is a dolphin-watching adventure tour in the Bahamas. Their photos and videos make me want to plan a vacation there.

In your own life traveling around, you have probably seen many attempts by merchants to entice you to Like their company.

Your Facebook URL should appear everywhere – business cards, posters, on vehicles, and even under your signature on every email are great spots to drive more visitors to your Facebook page and ideally generate more Likes. You can also create contests on your Facebook page to get more Likes. You can send emails to your customers asking them to Like your page. You just have to get started!

To improve the management of your Facebook page, one of the best tools out there is offered by Hootsuite.com. It allows you to create content and then the content will post on various social media accounts you have set up at a time that you select. This allows you to compose well-written

The Entrepreneur's Guide to Strategies, Secrets and Savings

posts when you have time, and yet get attention at an optimal time to reach new customers.

Advertising on Facebook – Another important feature of Facebook is an opportunity to advertise your business. You can set up one of those small ads you see when you visit Facebook. You can use demographics to specify which users will see your ad. For example, women between the ages of 40-50 with an interest in tennis, living within 25 miles of your business. It is a really great way to target your market. You can set your own small weekly budget and monitor the response. When you get new customers, ask them where they learned of your business. If they frequently answer Facebook, then you may want to increase your advertising budget.

Google+ offers similar opportunities and the differences are insignificant enough for new entrepreneurs to be left for a future date when you feel you have the time to manage two accounts.

Pay-Per-Click or PPC – You will hear these terms and they relate to paying for advertising. Google is probably the best known for this program. These programs are for businesses that need to drive inquiries and sales via the Internet.

In simple terms, when you search for information on a topic on Google, the "results page" will have both "organic" and "paid advertising" results. The paid ads will always say, "AD" or "ADS" beside them. They usually appear on the top and bottom and side of the page. Some sites will also use the words "Sponsored Content" as well as "ADS" beside paid ads.

Organic results are not paid for, and are intended to represent the most relevant and popular pages on the topic you have searched for.

BUSINESS, BUSINESS, BUSINESS!

You can easily buy ads on Google, Yahoo, and Bing. Frankly, Google will be enough for most entrepreneurs to handle at the beginning.

If your business needs more attention from potential customers, these ads can be a real boost for you, as long as you do it very carefully.

Go to adwords.google.com to get started. They have free phone support on weekdays. The number and details will be shown on their home page. I have always found their staff to be very helpful.

The general concept is this: You create a small ad that you think will be of interest to potential customers. Then you decide when you want the ad to be seen – maybe Monday to Friday from 8 a.m. to 5 p.m. Then you pick your geographical areas where you want your ad to be seen. Then you decide how much money you want to spend in a certain period – a week, a month, etc. Then I recommend you call Google and get their assistance with deciding on keywords – the words that will be used to cause your ads to appear in search engines and possibly some websites. Do not try and do this yourself the first time, as it is a surefire way to waste a lot of money and get very poor results. Review your settings with the Google representative, especially the demographic information to ensure it is optimized for your business.

Your ads will then be shown on the Internet until your budget is exhausted. It can happen faster than you expect. This is the importance of seeking assistance from a Google representative.

A strong word of caution – you can burn through a lot of money on Adwords. Yes, you can set a budget, but it is easy to increase your budget when your ads don't run since your

The Entrepreneur's Guide to Strategies, Secrets and Savings

initial money has run out. You must be careful to monitor where your new business comes from. If for $100 of Adwords spending your get $10,000 in new business, then that is a no-brainer – keep doing it. If your $100 only gets you $500 in new business, then you have to think carefully if the new business is really worth it. Did you spend all of your profits from the $500 in new sales on Adwords? Then you have done a lot of work for nothing.

Again, and I hate to repeat myself, but for some reason people always ignore this advice and try it themselves. Call Google at the number shown on the home page and ask for help from the experts. You will save a great deal of money and time. I have always found them to be fair and not just trying to get you to spend money.

There are many companies that will offer to run your Adwords program. Be careful. If you are a truly small company, then you should just call Google for help or find someone inexpensive on Elance.com. If you have grown to the point where you are able to hire an advertising agency with Adwords expertise, then by all means do so.

Do not get confused with the program called Adsense. It is a program where your website will have ads from other companies. It is not for you when you are setting out as a small business. Focus on building your business first.

Finally, you will find there are many social media sites and as a new business, you won't have time for them, unless they are really pertinent to generating new sales at the volume you need to succeed. Some of the major sites are Twitter, Instagram, and Pinterest. Unless you are truly computer literate, there will be a major learning curve to determine how these sites can best serve your purpose of increasing sales. I recommend you learn a little about each one as you have time.

Chapter Fourteen

Free Websites and Maximizing Their Effect

Obviously, a website is a must for every business and the kind I like are free and entirely suitable for a new small business. Your website will drive new revenue for your business if created and managed properly. The nature of websites is always evolving, and thus many consultants will oversell you just to line their pockets. There is no doubt that websites have become both an art and a science.

I was building websites when most people had never heard of them. I have some valuable tips to offer that I learned while creating hundreds of websites for myself. These tips will be valuable to new entrepreneurs and small businesses.

New style of websites – The appearance of websites is changing rapidly. Look at some of the sites I have referred to in this book and you will see single, large photos with a minimum of tabs and words, such as PipelineDeals.com, GotoMeeting.com, and Wix.com.

Getting started: If you have the time and patience, you can post a job on Elance.com and negotiate with providers to get exactly the website you want. Most new businesses can have a simple website created for under $500. However, if you create your own website, you will have many challenges when it comes to ecommerce transactions, including setting up a payment system for your customers.

Wix.com offers a great option for new and existing small businesses. More than 55 million clients use Wix.com. Wix.com offers terrific looking templates for many types of businesses. The templates are easy to customize and require no coding knowledge. This system is really quite simple and prices start at $4.08 per month. An ecommerce site costs $8.08 per month and includes a free domain name and $350 in gift vouchers to use for Google Adwords, Bing.com ads, Facebook ads, and on local listings. These prices

BUSINESS, BUSINESS, BUSINESS!

include hosting. There are no set-up fees and Google Analytics is part of every package they offer.

Godaddy.com offers a similar service to Wix.com. I use Godaddy.com for a variety of services and have been pleased. However, I have friends that have used Godaddy to create a website and it seems to take a long time, and my friends have not been satisfied because of delays. Maybe my friends have presented a particular challenge. I do agree with them that there is a lot of upselling for options that are not easily understood.

If you have a website now and it has an out-of-date look, I suggest you look into one of the above companies. You can leave your existing site up while you build a new site and then change over very quickly when you are ready.

Below is a checklist for creating a website, depending on your type of company:

- Be clear who you are and what product or service you are selling.

- Photos reflective of your business – These must be high quality or you are not portraying your company in the best light.

- Phone number – If you want your customers to be able to reach you, then make your phone number really obvious and on all pages if possible. Also, for your customers' convenience, add a Contact Us page with an email link.

- Address of your location – If you want people to visit your location, make it easy. Give directions from all major highways, airports, and train stations – whatever makes sense in your situation. Add a link to Google Maps or embed the map into your site. If you think it will be helpful, mention nearby landmarks such as a baseball park or a university.

- Ordering function – If you are selling products or services on your website, spend some time deciding on the best system for you. Wix.com or Godaddy.com can lead you through your options. I always recommend PayPal as an option since your customers don't have to give you their credit or debit card information. It is given to PayPal, who most people will trust more than your new business. This will also save you lots of hassle trying to set up credit card processing accounts with a bank.

- Employment section – Even if you are not hiring now, I recommend a tab at the bottom of your site to collect information in the event you suddenly need more staff. Post the type of jobs you would typically hire for.

- Icons with links to your social media accounts – Facebook, Twitter, Pinterest, Instagram, and LinkedIn. When your company is the right size, this step is necessary as part of your social media program. If you are not using some of these yet, then leave them for now. It is easy to add them later.

- Return visitors – Selling to repeat customers should be a goal. How do you get them to come back? One important method is to reach out to them by email or Facebook with a link to your website. Your email or Facebook feed should offer a discount or some other enticement to return and make another purchase. Another more basic way is to have a tool on your site or really interesting information. Sites like Houzz.com have many return visitors because there is so much useful information. Can you try to become an expert on products or information offered by your website? If you are selling luxurious handbags, perhaps you can become an expert on colors, seasonal changes, materials, and the best manufacturers. Ideally, whatever the product or service you are selling, you should try to become a leading expert.

- Images and videos – Fill your website with very rich, colorful, and stunning images and videos. These will give your site credibility and if your visitors feel good, they will stick around and buy your products. When building your website, use "web ready" photos, especially if you are in an area with slower Internet speeds. These images are a lower resolution that allows your web page to load faster.

- Content – If you are starting a service business, let's say a heating and air-conditioning business, then try to relate to the homeowners. Let them know your technicians have uniforms and identification, which suggests it is safe to allow this person in their home. Tell the customers that the technician will wear shoe covers over his street shoes to protect their carpets. Have lots of articles on the website about heating and air-conditioning to show you have a passion for the business. You want your potential customers to put trust in you to do the job required.

- If you are comfortable writing about your business, your employees, and maybe your family and community activities, this will provide great original content for your website.

- Make sure to include any logos of business or trade associations you may belong to. Also add the logos of manufacturers you represent. You should ask permission to use these, although they will usually be happy to provide these to you as you are selling their products.

- Include "Privacy Policy" and "Terms of Use" links. Search Google for templates and edit with your information.

- Google Analytics is an outstanding tool to see how your website is being used by clients. Wix.com offers this as part of their package. There is a learning curve, but it is essential data to have if you want to know how your website is helping your business. And, of course it suggests ways to improve your website. You will learn how long visitors stay on your website and even which page they leave on. You will want this information to convert visitors to sales.

Search Engine Optimization – Also known as SEO, this has become a complex and sophisticated part of building and promoting your website. The primary goal of SEO is to have your website appear on the first page of results on Google, Bing, Yahoo or other search engines. The first step usually is done in the source code, where you need a good title, description, and keywords. If you use a template from a company like Wix.com, Godaddy.com, or others, they make it much easier to do this first step. Wix.com will also add you to 100 online directories. However, there are steps like adding metatags and backlinks that are probably too difficult for new entrepreneurs. As time goes on, you will learn more about these valuable steps. I have found that in talking to the people at Wix.com and Godaddy.com that they will lead you through steps such as being indexed by Google, how to get backlinks, and other steps to have your website noticed.

Warning: Don't become obsessed with your website to the detriment of other sources of sales, unless your only source is your website. There are companies that will offer to sell you backlinks to your website and "Likes" for Facebook. These are shady tactics and can get you into trouble with some search engines. Don't respond to random

BUSINESS, BUSINESS, BUSINESS!

emails offering services. Anybody that helps you will need your access codes, so the people behind the random emails will probably hold you hostage in the future.

Finally, there are fine companies on Elance.com that can handle your SEO at very reasonable prices. Just check out their references from past clients, make sure they have done lots of projects for others, and that they have a high overall rating from past clients. SEO is not a one-time event, but rather should occur constantly, so be prepared to pay a monthly fee for SEO.

Chapter Fifteen

Finding Overseas Suppliers

I always buy American-made goods if I can; however, as an entrepreneur, I recognize that keeping costs down is first and foremost if a business is to succeed. Competitors buy from China, so entrepreneurs in America and elsewhere in the world are forced to do so if they want to keep their doors open.

These days, you can buy or manufacture almost anything in China. Apple iPhones are made in China. Probably the computer you are using is made in China. Most of your garments – underwear, socks, t-shirts – are all made in China.

There was a time when merchandise made in China was questionable, but now the quality can be very high. Chinese companies will try very hard to meet your quality expectations, if you are clear at the outset. For those who think of some bad Chinese-made dog treats or gypsum drywall that has been mentioned in the media, you should be fair and acknowledge that in America, we occasionally have problems with a rogue businessperson selling bad beef, chicken, or other products.

I have visited small manufacturing facilities in China and been very impressed by the enthusiasm of not only the owner, but the staff as well. The owners have mortgages on their buildings, staff to pay, vehicles to insure, and raw materials to buy, just like many American companies. I have been impressed with their integrity and desire to earn my business.

There are sales and manufacturing facilities in China that you will never believe unless you see them with your own eyes. Two examples:

Yiwu Market (also known as Yiwu International Trade City) in Yiwu – this massive, sprawling complex has five

BUSINESS, BUSINESS, BUSINESS!

huge buildings totaling 25 million square feet. There are 80,000 merchants in the market with up to 200,000 buyers showing up most days. And, the market is open almost 365 days a year, closing only for the Spring Festival.

Buyers come from all over the world for everything imaginable – candles, photo frames, hair extensions, shoes, socks, kitchen products, and tourist gift shop items.

The other example is Swimwear City in Xingcheng under the administration of Huludao City. There are 350 swimwear manufacturers with 50,000 employees. The 150 million swimsuits that these companies produce annually represent one-third of China's production.

Both Yiwu Market and Swimsuit City have very enthusiastic merchants wanting to do business with you. And if these markets don't meet your needs, there are many others throughout China that have merchants who want your business. It is best to time your visit with major trade shows to get the most out of your trip to China. The Canton Fair is the big event and takes place in the Spring and Autumn each year. However, most merchants want to deal in only very large purchases and it is very expensive for hotels and flights. It is my opinion that new entrepreneurs and small businesses would not benefit from visiting the Canton Fair, but should focus on areas of China that have smaller fairs and that meet their specific needs.

That said, I still believe you must be very careful in how you proceed. Some advice before you go to China:

Do extensive research for the products you want to buy or manufacture. Some of the largest websites can offer thousands of products for your consideration. In some cases, they will retail small quantities and in others, large

The Entrepreneur's Guide to Strategies, Secrets and Savings

orders are required. Some reputable websites worthy of your research are:

- Alibaba.com – two million storefronts with 45 million members in 190 countries
- AliExpress.com – offers easy shipment to the U.S. and takes most forms of payment

While the following companies are smaller, they have some really amazing opportunities to buy products made in China that you can re-sell in North America.

– DHGate.com

– LightintheBox.com

– EternalBuy.com

– ChinaBot.com

– SearchingPanda.com

– Biz-with-China.com

– FreeShoppingChina.com

– YoungMoneyChina.com

You will need to arrange a visa to visit China. The rules can be complex and will require a visit by you to a Chinese Embassy unless you use a Passport Expediting Firm. There are many on the Internet.

In Shanghai and Beijing, I suggest you stay in an American or Canadian branded hotel. Many employees speak fluent English and can really make your travels much easier. Depending on your personal standards, there are very inexpensive hotels like the Best Western and Ramada

BUSINESS, BUSINESS, BUSINESS!

chains with rooms often as low as $35 U.S., as well as luxury hotels such as the Four Seasons and Fairmont hotels.

High speed trains make travel easy between major cities. For example, Shanghai to Yiwu takes 2.5 hours.

Taxis are inexpensive by American standards.

Plan to stay 10-14 days if you are going to more than one city. The reason for a stay this long is that you will want to arrange meetings with at least three agents. These agents will represent your interests while you are back in America tending to your business.

There are plenty of agents with amazing websites promising the moon, and not much else going for them, so you must do your due diligence.

- For example, if you go to Yiwu Market, you will want to spend the morning walking the market with the agent.

- Observe how many merchants the agent knows and if he is welcomed or not.

- Does the agent have contacts with the type of manufacturers or suppliers you need? Of course you have asked this question before you agreed to meet the agent, but you will want to verify this for yourself on your visit.

- In the afternoon, visit their office and their manufacturing facilities to see for yourself that you are dealing with the owner, or at least that the owner greets you.

- Ask for names of American or Canadian companies that you can contact for reference verification.

- Ask for copies of their company ID, tax registration, and business license. Be sure to obtain their Chinese name, as most Chinese take a name like Bill, Luke, Mary, or Brenda to make it easier for you. If there is a problem and the authorities need to be contacted, you will need the correct Chinese name.

- As you view their facility, make sure it meets your needs. Does the facility have room to repackage your goods if necessary? Is there room to hold goods from various suppliers until you have enough to fill a container? Can the agent fill a container at their facility and can it be picked up by a truck?

- At Yiwu Market, only about 30% of the shops do their own manufacturing, so be prepared to wait 3-30 days for your order to be ready for shipping.

- Merchants do not take credit cards. You should arrive in China with sufficient cash to make deposits. Carrying cash in China is common and generally safe. Remember to make declarations of unspent cash on return to the U.S. if the amount exceeds $10,000. You can withdraw cash at ATMs at Yiwu Market, however the machines may have a limit different than what your card is approved for in the U.S. Once you have made a deposit on a purchase, the balance can usually be wired or sent by Western Union.

- Good agents will spend time with you on the phone, Skype, and email to answer your questions before arrival in China. Visit Yiwu-Market-Guide.com for the contact information of a well-respected agent.

A local buyer's agent is really important in order for you to have a successful first buying trip to China. They charge a commission based on the purchase price of goods and other services they provide. Since each agent sets his or her own commission, check before hiring the agent. As mentioned earlier, even if the agent has been very helpful before your departure, meet and interview at least three agents on your arrival in China.

These are the services you can expect an agent to perform for you:

- Introduce you to suppliers
- Assist you with placing orders
- Pay deposits
- Follow production
- Do quality control by sampling at least 10% of production on a random basis
- If you have purchased from various suppliers, your agent must be willing to load into one container
- Prepare Customs papers
- Do Customs declarations
- Send you customers' copies of paperwork to help clear your container when it arrives in the U.S.
- Follow-up communication with suppliers as needed.

If you are able to order from a supplier on Alibaba.com, your task will be much easier and safer. Alibaba has identified some suppliers as Gold Suppliers. These Gold Suppliers have lots of extra support from Alibaba, which will help protect you. This support includes an escrow service so that your funds are held until the supplier performs. Alibaba has also performed a verification service by visiting the manufacturing facilities of Gold Suppliers. They also offer a Sea Freight Service. I recommend you visit Alibaba.com for full details on their programs.

The downside of using Alibaba.com is that the prices from merchants are usually higher than you could negotiate for yourself by dealing directly with a manufacturer. You must do a cost-benefit analysis and factor in the cost of

The Entrepreneur's Guide to Strategies, Secrets and Savings

traveling to China, hotel and other travel costs in China, the cost of an agent, and the cost to your business of being away from the U.S.

Even though buying in China can seem complicated, the fact is that you can buy at very low prices and get products of reasonable to very high quality depending on the products you are seeking.

I recommend a small test order with a supplier before committing to a container. If you receive a container of inferior quality products from China, you have little recourse if you buy directly. This is where an agent who does random quality sampling is so valuable. You will also learn if the supplier can perform even on a small order. Yes, the costs of shipping a small order will be higher; however, you will be risking a lot less.

Finally, I recommend ordering far in advance of when you will need the product. Using big manufacturers, you might be competing with large American stores for product. You don't have to think too hard as to who gets the merchandise first.

As well, each year there are many stories of how backlogged shipping ports and related facilities can be near Christmas and other holidays. As I write this paragraph, there is an article, by Andrew Khouri in the *Los Angeles Times* newspaper on this problem. An excerpt:

"The twin ports of Los Angeles and Long Beach are experiencing a logistical nightmare as they struggle to ease a bottleneck that could undermine retailers' all important holiday shopping season...

BUSINESS, BUSINESS, BUSINESS!

"In the worst shipping crisis in a decade, mammoth vessels loaded with products destined for the nation's stores are sitting idle just off the coast..."

The article is accompanied by a photo of containers described as "a mountain of cargo containers."

Again, plan ahead and order well in advance. The cost of some extra warehouse time to have your products near your office is cheap compared to the aggravation of your product being tied up on a dock somewhere.

The basic issues described here about buying from China apply in similar ways to purchasing from Vietnam, India, Indonesia, Bangladesh, and other countries.

Chapter Sixteen

An Exit Plan and Some Interesting Choices

We entrepreneurs are odd people as a rule. We are excited to launch our business and watch as customers buy our products and services. We have a myriad of personal goals that will define success for us.

Likewise, depending on our age and stage in life, we all see our exit from our business differently.

As entrepreneurs, it is often the challenge of building our business that excites us, and not the ongoing management. We call it boredom when we begin to run a "cookie-cutter" business. Steady income just isn't enough. For those of us who fit this description, we just want to maximize the dollars we get out of the business so we can move on to the next idea.

It doesn't take much imagination to know someone seeking to sell his business at 25 years of age will have vastly different objectives than someone 65 years of age.

And, if we set an exit strategy as soon as we start building our new business, we may be setting ourselves up to fail. Often when I am approached by a young entrepreneur, their emphasis is on all the money they will make when they sell the business. They make no secret of this approach. However, if their employees know that this is the goal, they will be demoralized from the first day and the young entrepreneur will probably never grow his company. You cannot build a company if you and your employees have opposing dreams. In the launch of a new Internet business, it is common to issue stock to employees as a strategy to build some loyalty. However, worthless stock certificates litter the Silicon Valley, San Francisco, Los Angeles, New York, and many other "startup" cities. Success stories are rare, but great when they happen.

BUSINESS, BUSINESS, BUSINESS!

So, in my opinion, after a business has been launched and success is ongoing, then is the time to plan an exit strategy. I have identified three common options, supported by many financial planners and accountants.

1. Exit every day. Operate a lifestyle company and take as much cash out for yourself as possible. Buy a nice car every year, take exotic vacations, and live life as you want. The big downside is that you will probably pay more taxes on income now rather than on capital gains in the future. Obviously, this will not work if you have investors who have not been paid back in full or partners with a different approach. If you are the sole shareholder, and want to live this life, then be generous to your employees to nurture the loyalty that you need to continue operating your "lifestyle" business. Don't spend all you take out. Invest some in real estate or the stock market to try and have funds for when you are no longer able to work.

2. Liquidate the business. Build your business as well as you can and one day liquidate. I know several people who just became overwhelmed with the business and personal affairs and suddenly decided to liquidate their business and move to another country where they believed their life would be stress free. I have visited Costa Rica many times and always end up meeting American, Canadian, Swiss, German, and French expats. Some were just fed up with being on the freeway back home for 2-4 hours a day. Some were tired of the stress of getting enough sales to pay the bills. I have met former electrical contractors, dentists, farmers, Internet company executives, home builders, and many others. For the most part, once they made the decision to close their business, all staff was terminated, all assets sold for as much as possible, accounts receivables collected, and accounts payable paid. They put the cash in the bank and live a much less expensive life. The downside

to this approach is the loss of the goodwill in the business and getting fire-sale prices for assets instead of market value. There are probably negative tax consequences as well.

3. Plan for a sale, a merger, or an acquisition. Once you have a business generating steady profits, then it is time to plan a professional exit strategy. Confidentially, over time, consult with your financial planner, accountant, and tax attorney to learn your options. Keep this quiet at the office. If one person knows you are planning an exit, soon everyone will know. You will want to have a smooth transition; maintain the value of your business; reduce tax consequences; ensure income for your retirement; and leave a strategic vision for the new operator of your business.

Three things to avoid to ensure the sale, merger, or acquisition of your company:

1. For the three years prior to sale, make sure you don't have any lifestyle expenses on your books, such as vacations, car payments, family meals out, and personal insurance as you want to increase EBITDA as significantly as possible to maximize the price you get for your company.

2. Eliminate the potential of any lawsuits. Unresolved lawsuits represent unknown liability to buyers and if they decide to proceed anyway, they will probably insist on lowering their purchase price or being indemnified in some other way.

3. Eliminate any accounting issues. Personal loans to you or family member, unpaid taxes, and overdue suppliers all are big red flags to potential buyers.

You are blessed to be an entrepreneur and to live an exceptional life making choices and having the personal

BUSINESS, BUSINESS, BUSINESS!

time and freedom to live every day as you wish. Think of your exit plan as a wonderful transition to a new opportunity.

Appendix A – Domain Names and Owners Referenced in BUSINESS, BUSINESS, BUSINESS!

The following is a list of domain names, or URLs, that are provided to make it easy for readers to obtain information about the products or services of businesses mentioned in this book. All brand names, product names, Registered names or Trademarks are used for journalistic or editorial purposes only, and belong to their respective owners. BUSINESS, BUSINESS, BUSINESS! has no ownership and does not intend to imply any relationship. Mentioned companies and their URLs:

Adwords.google.com

Affirm.com

Alibaba.com

AliExpress.com

Amazon.com

AngelCapitalAssociation.org/directory

AngelResourceGroup.org

Avvo.com

Bing.com

Biz-with-China.com

Boxpark.co.uk

BuildaSign.com

CheapDoorHangers.com

BUSINESS, BUSINESS, BUSINESS!

ChinaBot.com

Codecademy.com

ConstantContact.com

Contracts.onecle.com

Craigslist.org

CreditCardProcessing.com

CrossCampus.us

DHGate.com

DocuSign.com

DowntownContainerPark.com

EternalBuy.com

Etsy.com

Facebook.com

FreelancersUnion.org

FreeShoppingChina.com

FundingCircle.com

Github.com

Global.alipay.com

Godaddy.com

GoFundMe.com

Google.com/alerts

The Entrepreneur's Guide to Strategies, Secrets and Savings

Googleforentrepreneurs.com

GotoMeeting.com

Hootsuite.com

Houzz.com

Hubspot.com

Indiegogo.com

Instagram.com

Intracen.org

KhanAcademy.org

Kickstarter.com

LegalZoom.com

LendingClub.com

LightintheBox.com

LinkedIn.com

Marketo.com

Meetup.com

Nolo.com

OpenTable.com

Paypal.com

Pinterest.com

PipelineDeals.com

BUSINESS, BUSINESS, BUSINESS!

Prosper.com

Proxysf.net

PRWeb.com

RocketLawyer.com

Salesforce.com

SCORE.org/mentors

SearchingPanda.com

Shopify.com

Squareup.com

StartupNY.com

Techshop.ws

Thomasnet.com

TripAdvisor.com

Twitter.com

Upstart.com

USPTO.gov/inventors/patents

Vistaprint.com

Wix.com

Wonderlic.com

Yahoo.com

Yelp.com

The Entrepreneur's Guide to Strategies, Secrets and Savings

Yiwu-Market-Guide.com

YoungMoneyChina.com

YouTube.com

Zappos.com

ZipRecruiter.com

Appendix B – Example of SWOP Analysis

The following SWOP Analysis was prepared by a new entrepreneur analyzing the viability of an online lingerie business. It demonstrates how simple a SWOP analysis can be and is intended to help a new entrepreneur make the correct decisions. Note that since this analysis was for her own purposes there is no professional format required – just the Strengths, Weaknesses, Operations, and Profitability as seen by her.

SWOP Analysis: MirasCloset.com

STRENGTHS:

- Quality products, personally picked by me, directly from the manufacturer

- Business knowledge of the owner

- Differentiation – new styles not available in market

- Personal interest in lingerie

- Bilingual offer - .cz, .com and other domains

- Affordable investment

- Can support cash demands, if necessary, of business for at least two years

- Lower prices possible than competitors' offering

WEAKNESSES:

- Competition from other websites

- Lingerie website not being new on market

- Missing "dressing rooms" where customers would normally be able to try on

- My low skills with respect to websites

- Overseas suppliers and import difficulties

- Challenge to fill a gap in market with a new style of existing product

- Trying to be different with better product and website quality

- Possibility of miscalculating customers´ taste and needs

- Big brands have existing online stores

- Possibility of weak demand

- Finding and building relationship with Chinese supplier

OPERATIONS:

- Minimal storage space needed for boxes of imported lingerie

- I can re-package lingerie from China into individual packages for re-mailing to customers

- As demand grows, lots of low-cost potential employees to do re-packaging

- Minimal re-labeling

- Can update website myself

BUSINESS, BUSINESS, BUSINESS!

- Travel to China, probably annually to source suppliers

PROFITABILITY:

- Buy in China to start and get low prices
- High mark-up at retail
- Low operating costs – storage of $180 per month
- My personal health insurance - $200
- Labeling -Need 1000 labels to place on each product cover -Estimated $100

- Start-up costs in quick view:
- Website: up to $1,500
- Inventory (including shipping, duty): up to $3,000
- Images for website: up to $500
- Marketing: suggested $500 for the beginning
- Total of suggested start-up expenses....$6,000

Fixed costs

- To be paid every month, not depending on sales
    - Insurance: $200
    - Storage: $180
    - Marketing tools: $250
- Total of fixed costs: $630

Variable costs

- To be variable, depending on sales
    - Photocopy/print

- Cell phone
- Label print
- Postage
- Gas/car
- -Packaging
- -Other
- Total of estimated variable costs paid monthly: $200

Break-even Analysis

- Break point should be reached in month 7 from starting selling
- Lower sales expectations
- Calculation for 12 months
- Calculating with fixed and estimated variable expenses
- For more details see Excel sheet called "Financial Plan Attachment"
- "Profit or Loss 12 months" sheet one

Selling Price calculation

- Calculated on 140% margin
- Average selling price of $20/ piece (set of bra and panties)

Minimum sales calculation

- To cover fixed and estimated variable costs must sell a minimum of 38 sets/mon
- Calculated with average selling price of $20
- Reasonable amount, should be easy to achieve
- Lower sales expectations in the beginning, costs of first six months must be covered

BUSINESS, BUSINESS, BUSINESS!

Sales goal per month – grow each month with goal of 150 sets by month 12, based on repeat and referral business as well as new website and social media marketing. Average of 75 sets per month. First 38 sets cover all costs. Next 37 sets with a profit of $16 each or average profit of $600 per month for first year.

Second year, average of 225 sets per month. First 45 sets a month to cover costs. Next 180 sets at a profit of $16 each would yield an average profit per month of $2,880 per month.

Profit in second year of $34,000. Paid to me as owner.

Years 3-5: Expect growth to continue. Review cost and profit estimates 2x year from day one.

Appendix C – Test for Prospective Employees

The purpose of this test is to do a basic assessment of an <u>entry-level</u> prospective employee. It will assist employers to understand the areas where an applicant has the strongest skills, and their level of logic for problem solving.

Prospective Employees General Business Skills

Name_____Score_____Date_____

1. ODDITY   AUDIT Are these words:
   a. Similar
   b. Opposite
   c. Neither   _____

2. Arrange the following words to make a sentence. Print the LAST letter of the last word as the answer.

   DOGS RAINED AND IT CATS   _____

3. PLEASANT is the opposite of:
   a. Happy
   b. Nice
   c. Friendly
   d. Surly
   e. Contented   _____

4. The eighth month of the year is:
   a. April
   b. September
   c. August   _____

BUSINESS, BUSINESS, BUSINESS!

5. In the following list of words, which is different?
   a. Daisy
   b. Aster
   c. Tulip
   d. Flower
   e. Rose   _____

6. AWFUL UNLAWFUL Are these words:
   a. Similar
   b. Opposite
   c. Neither   _____

7. DIRTY is the opposite of:
   a. Sordid
   b. Unclean
   c. Filthy
   d. Soiled
   e. Purged   _____

8. Accepting that (1) and (2) are true, is (1)
   a. True
   b. False
   c. Not sure   _____

   1. Blondes have more fun
   2. Anne is a blonde
   3. She has more fun

9. Are the meanings of the following
   a. Similar
   b. Opposite
   c. Neither   _____

   -Six of one, half a dozen of the other.

200

The Entrepreneur's Guide to Strategies, Secrets and Savings

-Pay your money, take your choice.

10. How many of the pairs of numbers listed below are exact duplicates?

    7.71   7.77
    12.74   14.72
    44471   44471
    12344   12134
    171172   171174   _____

11. In the following list of words, which is different?

    a. Orange
    b. Apple
    c. Pear
    d. Fruit
    e. Peach   _____

12. DISSENT is the opposite of

    a. Disagree
    b. Assent
    c. Doubt
    d. Differ
    e. Protest   _____

13. Jelly beans sell at 3 for $0.15.

    How much will 1.5 dozen cost?   _____

14. What number should come next in the following sequence?

    8 - 4 - 2 - 1 - ½ - ¼   _____

15. A car travels 60 ft. in 1/5 second. At this speed, how many feet can it travel in 3 seconds? _____

BUSINESS, BUSINESS, BUSINESS!

16. IDLE IDYLLIC are these words
    a. Similar
    b. Opposite
    c. Neither   _____

17. Pins sell at 10 for $0.25.

    How much will 1 ½ dozen cost?   _____

18. In the following list of words, which is different from the others?
    a. Tea
    b. Drink
    c. Coffee
    d. Milk
    e. Wine   _____

19. ABSOLVE ABJECT are these words
    a. Similar
    b. Opposite
    c. Not sure   _____

20. Two of the following proverbs have the same meaning. Which ones?
    a. All things come to he who waits.
    b. Experience is a great teacher.
    c. One bitten, twice shy.
    d. Patience is a virtue.
    e. Hitch your wagon to a star.   _____

21. Jack sold 25 cars last month. That was 5/8 of his quota. What was his quota?   _____

22. Accepting (a) and (b) are true, is (c)

The Entrepreneur's Guide to Strategies, Secrets and Savings

1. True
2. False
3. Not sure

   a. Normal boys are active and mischievous.
   b. Bob is a normal boy.
   c. Bob is mischievous.   _____

23. OBESE is the opposite of
   a. Abscess
   b. Ornate
   c. Corpulent
   d. Gaunt
   e. Purged   _____

24. Which of the following represents the largest amount?

   .8   .888   .96   .189   .89   _____

25. VERSATILE   VERSE are these words
   a. Similar
   b. Opposite
   c. Neither   _____

26. Arrange and write the following words in a sentence. If it is a true statement, mark T in the accompanying blank; if it is a false, mark F.

   rain   Snow   frozen   is

_____

   _____

27. A baseball player has a batting average of 20%. How many times must he bat to register 200 hits?

   _____

BUSINESS, BUSINESS, BUSINESS!

28. In the following sets of words, which is different from the others?

   a. Sugar
   b. Honey
   c. Syrup
   d. Sweet
   e. Jam   _____

29. Which number is out of pattern in the following series?

   1 ¼   ¾   1/3   ¼   -1/4   _____

30. REPROACH   REBUKE   Are these works
   a. Similar
   b. Opposite
   c. Neither   _____

Prospective Employees General Business Skills

Answer Key

1. ODDITY AUDIT Are these words:
   a. Similar
   b. Opposite
   c. Neither   ___C___

2. Arrange the following words to make a sentence. Print the LAST letter of the last word as the answer.

   DOGS RAINED AND IT CATS   ___S___

3. PLEASANT is the opposite of:
   a. Happy
   b. Nice
   c. Friendly
   d. Surly
   e. Contented   ___D___

4. The eighth month of the year is:
   a. April
   b. September
   c. August   ___C___

5. In the following list of words, which is different?
   a. Daisy
   b. Aster
   c. Tulip
   d. Flower
   e. Rose   ___D___

BUSINESS, BUSINESS, BUSINESS!

6. AWFUL UNLAWFUL Are these words:

   a. Similar
   b. Opposite
   c. Neither   ____C____

7. DIRTY is the opposite of:

   a. Sordid
   b. Unclean
   c. Filthy
   d. Soiled
   e. Purged   ____E____

8. Accepting that (1) and (2) are true, is (1)

   a. True
   b. False
   c. Not sure

   1. Blondes have more fun
   2. Anne is a blonde
   3. She has more fun   ____A (T)____

9. Are the meanings of the following

   a. Similar
   b. Opposite
   c. Neither   ____C____

   -Six of one, half a dozen of the other.
   -Pay your money, take your choice.

10. How many of the pairs of numbers listed below are exact duplicates?

7.71	7.77
12.74	14.72
44471	44471

The Entrepreneur's Guide to Strategies, Secrets and Savings

    12344   12134
    171172   171174   ___1___

11. In the following list of words, which is different?

    a. Orange
    b. Apple
    c. Pear
    d. Fruit
    e. Peach   ___D___

12. DISSENT is the opposite of

    a. Disagree
    b. Assent
    c. Doubt
    d. Differ
    e. Protest   ___B___

13. Jelly beans sell at 3 for $0.15.
    How much will 1.5 dozen cost?   ___.90___

14. What number should come next in the following sequence?

    8 - 4 - 2 - 1 - ½ - ¼   ___1/8___

15. A car travels 60 ft. in 1/5 second. At this speed, how many feet can it travel in 3 seconds?   _900 FT_

16. IDLE IDYLLIC are these words

    a. Similar
    b. Opposite
    c. Neither   ___C___

BUSINESS, BUSINESS, BUSINESS!

17. Pins sell at 10 for $0.25.

    How much will 1 ½ dozen cost?   _0.45_

18. In the following list of words, which is different from the others?

    a. Tea
    b. Drink
    c. Coffee
    d. Milk
    e. Wine   __B__

19. ABSOLVE   ABJECT are these words

    a. Similar
    b. Opposite
    c. Not sure   __B__

20. Two of the following proverbs have the same meaning. Which ones?

    a. All things come to he who waits.
    b. Experience is a great teacher.
    c. One bitten, twice shy.
    d. Patience is a virtue.
    e. Hitch your wagon to a star.   __A AND D__

21. Jack sold 25 cars last month. That was 5/8 of his quota. What was his quota?   __40__

22. Accepting (a) and (b) are true, is (c)

    1. True
    2. False
    3. Not sure

    a. Normal boys are active and mischievous.
    b. Bob is a normal boy.

208

The Entrepreneur's Guide to Strategies, Secrets and Savings

   c. Bob is mischievous.   ____1 (T)___

23. OBESE is the opposite of
    a. Abscess
    b. Ornate
    c. Corpulent
    d. Gaunt
    e. Purged   ____D____

24. Which of the following represents the largest amount?
    .8 .888 .96 .189 .89   ___.96___

25. VERSATILE   VERSE are these words
    a. Similar
    b. Opposite
    c. Neither   ____C____

26. Arrange and write the following words in a sentence. If it is a true statement, mark T in the accompanying blank; if it is a false, mark F.

      rain   Snow   frozen   is

    Snow is frozen rain._____
                                  ____T____

27. A baseball player has a batting average of 20%. How many times must he bat to register 200 hits?
                              __1000__

28. In the following sets of words, which is different from the others?
    a. Sugar
    b. Honey
    c. Syrup

BUSINESS, BUSINESS, BUSINESS!

    d. Sweet
    e. Jam   ___D___

29. Which number is out of pattern in the following series?

    1 ¼   ¾   1/3   ¼   -1/4   ___1/3___

30. REPROACH   REBUKE   Are these works
    a. Similar
    b. Opposite
    c. Neither   ___A___

www.ingramcontent.com/pod-product-compliance
Lightning Source LLC
Chambersburg PA
CBHW051642170526
45167CB00001B/299